VICTORIA FALLS
& SURROUNDS
THE INSIDER'S GUIDE

VICTORIA FALLS &
THE INSIDER'S GUIDE

CONTENTS

AUTHOR'S NOTE

This book, the fourth in *The Insider's Guide* series, while focused on Victoria Falls, also covers a selection of appealing destinations in Zimbabwe, Zambia and Botswana that are found within reasonably close proximity.

I dedicate this work to the Zimbabwean people who have stayed and battled so bravely to keep their country from the abyss. Over the last seven years, a period that for many has been the country's darkest and most trying, I have paid annual visits. While each trip brought deeper levels of sadness and anguish, there were pockets of hope as I witnessed the Herculean labours of the extraordinary people who keep the place going. It has always been written on their faces and seen in the fortitude of their will that someday soon they will reclaim this truly magnificent country from its tyranny.

Ian Michler, a stockbroker by profession, left the world of finance in 1989 to live and work in the Okavango Delta, where he also owned a lodge for a period of time. He has 16 years of guiding experience – mostly in Botswana, Namibia, Zimbabwe, Zambia and East Africa – conducting big game, birding, adventure and photographic safaris. When not on safari, he works as a photojournalist, writing on conservation, wildlife, and travel issues, predominantly for *Africa Geographic* and *Africa – Birds and Birding*. Ian has five previous books to his credit: the three *Insider's Guides*: *Botswana*, *Zanzibar* and *Kenya & Tanzania*, as well as *This is Mozambique* and *Mozambique – A Visual Souvenir*. He is a past category winner in the Agfa Wildlife Photographic Awards. Ian is presently based in Cape Town, South Africa, where he is a partner in a safari company offering specialist guided trips.

To travel with Ian as your guide or receive advice on travel in Southern or East Africa, you can contact him at:

INVENT AFRICA   Tel: +27 21 7011179
e-mail: reservations@inventafrica.com
website: www.inventafrica.com

It has been with the assistance and support of others that I have been able to complete this project. My sincere thanks and gratitude go to them for their generous efforts: in Zimbabwe, Rob and Barry Style and their families from Buffalo Range; Yvonne Christian, Ron Goatley, Courteney Johnson and Keith Vincent of Wilderness Safaris; Shane White, Craig White and Floyd Ambrose of Wild Horizons; Phathisani Nkomo of Shearwater Adventures; Charles Kamseka of The Stanley and Livingstone; Rabhelani Moyo of the Victoria Falls Hotel; Dana Heath of Victoria Falls Safari Lodge; Gail Webster, Des Van Jaarsveld and Steve Bolnick of Jedsons Wilderness Camp; Rolf Steiner and Peter Gava of CC Africa; Sanele Dhlomo.

In Zambia, Ali Shenton; Howard and Sheri Shackleton of Shackletons Upper Zambezi Lodge; Faan and Ann-Marie Fourie of Taita Falcon Lodge; Richard Sheppard of Fawlty Towers; Graham Nel of The Waterfront; Nico Chassing of Bundu Adventures; Batoka Sky, Mark and Tanya Stephens of Islands of Siankaba; Honour Schram de Jong of Tongabezi Lodge and Sindabezi Island.

In Botswana, Brian Gardiner and Ryan Powell of Sanctuary Lodges; Jonathan Gibson of Desert & Delta; Simon Blackburn of Kwando Safaris; Peter and Salome Comley.

And to Colin Bell for his assistance; Mike Myers and Courteney Johnson for their fantastic photographs; and Tessa van Schaik for the awesome maps.

Page 1: *A kayaker prepares to tackle rapid 2, Zambezi Gorge.* **Pages 2–3:** *Victoria Falls, one of the Seven Natural Wonders of the World.* **Pages 4–5:** *The Zambezi River, upstream of the Victoria Falls.* **Opposite:** *Good Samaritan Café, popular with locals in Livingstone.*

Welcome to

VICTORIA FALLS &

SURROUNDS

Africa is world renowned for its numerous **iconic geographical features**: Ngorongoro Crater, Table Mountain, the Okavango Delta and Mt Kilimanjaro would make an appearance on most people's lists. But a certainty, and possibly even the most celebrated of all would have to be **Victoria Falls**, the world's most impressive waterfall and one of the Seven Natural Wonders of the World. Lying almost exactly central in the southern half of the continent and close to where four countries, Botswana, Zimbabwe, Zambia and Namibia meet, its convenient location adds to its accessibility, making it one of the most visited sites on the continent.

It was Dr David Livingstone who in 1855 announced the presence of Victoria Falls to the outside world. Cecil John Rhodes, arriving decades later, made them accessible by building the first railway line from the south and then commissioning the bridge across the Zambezi River that still stands today. They both marvelled at what they saw. Since then, the site has attracted an ever-increasing number of visitors, supporting a substantial tourism industry in both Victoria Falls town in Zimbabwe and Livingstone in Zambia. Victoria Falls serves as a feature attraction for visitors travelling anywhere in Southern Africa.

While the waterfall may be the highlight, the greater region has plenty of appealing sideshows. Upstream and downstream, the Zambezi offers a multitude of exciting options, and both Zambia and Zimbabwe have a choice of magnificent national parks and reserves. A mere 70 kilometres to the west, the Chobe River and the Chobe National Park in Botswana form the third sector of what is in effect a regional safari destination as rewarding as any.

To those in doubt as to whether they should be travelling to Zimbabwe, the answer remains, 'Yes!' The country has gone through its bleakest period, brought on by a land reform programme that has nearly destroyed its political and economic fabric (see 'Land reform in Zimbabwe' below), but despite these upheavals, Zimbabwe remains a relatively safe place to travel. The land reform issues and the related incidents of violence have remained confined to the farms and amongst supporters of the government and the opposition Movement for Democratic Change.

With resources stretched, personnel limited and stamina tested, those keeping the tourism industry going and the national parks and conservancies intact need all the support they can get. The government is simply not capable, or willing, to provide these services as they should. To travel to **Zimbabwe today** is not to support Mugabe's regime, but rather to ensure he does not destroy everything. Every tourist dollar counts in the effort. Although there has been a substantial loss of wildlife in some conservancies due to poaching associated with the land invasions, the national parks have remained almost totally unaffected, with most still carrying large and healthy populations of wild animals. Zimbabwe has of course lost a substantial chunk of its tourism market, but while working under trying conditions, most tourism operators and facilities are still open for business. They have shown immense fortitude and resourcefulness in dealing with shortages and restrictions. If you are unsure about visiting, ask your travel advisor for a country update before you make your decision.

Zimbabwe's loss has been **Zambia's gain**, as Livingstone, a mere 10 kilometres away on the opposite side of the river, has experienced something of a boom in its tourism fortunes. With Zambia as a whole already on an upward path since the country's first multiparty elections in 1991, the Zimbabwe crisis for many has not meant missing out on a visit to Victoria Falls. Instead, it has simply been a case of changing destinations, from Zimbabwe to Zambia. With this substantial spillover adding weight to Livingstone's resurgence, investment is growing and goods and services are now readily and reasonably efficiently available. The town and its inhabitants are vibrant and upbeat about the future.

Botswana, more specifically its far northeastern border town of Kasane, and the nearby Chobe National Park, make up the third point in this regional triangle of tourism. Based on a multiparty democracy that has brought peace, stability and substantial economic progress to its people, Botswana is one of **Africa's great success** stories and is often referred to as the 'Switzerland of Africa'.

Together, it is a region offering an incredible diversity of thrilling destinations and is well worth visiting. Welcome to Victoria Falls and its supporting acts!

Dr David Livingstone (1813–1873)

Of the many European missionaries and explorers who travelled the African continent, staking the claims of their respective home countries during the nineteenth century, none has received more **acclaim and recognition** than David Livingstone. His numerous exploratory trips, spanning 33 years of travel, were instrumental in opening up and mapping the interior of southern and central Africa. For many, his Christian based anti-slavery campaign and his humanity are regarded as his most enduring legacies.

Born in Blantyre, Scotland on 19 March 1813 to parents who were devout Christians, he was the second oldest of seven children, brought up in humble conditions. Living in a tenement home amongst the cotton-mills of the region, Livingstone had to work the mills as a teenager while pursuing his school studies at night. Along with his Christian beliefs, these early years of hardship are likely to have been instrumental in his choosing a career combining missionary work with that of medicine. In his early twenties, he enrolled at various colleges in Glasgow, where he completed his medical studies as well as taking classes in Greek mythology, among other topics. He later joined the London Missionary Society and it was here that he met Dr Robert Moffat. After attending one of Moffat's seminars, Livingstone was persuaded that his future work should be in Africa rather than China, the country he had originally set his heart on.

And so it was that in 1840 he set sail for the Cape of Good Hope in South Africa, on his first trip abroad, where he soon began working at Moffat's Kuruman Mission in the dry hinterlands of the Northern Cape. It was work that thrilled him and in an environment that inspired him, it was not long before he had learnt his first African language and begun establishing his own mission posts north of Kuruman. It was also here that he met his future wife, Mary Moffat, the daughter of Dr Robert Moffat.

Driven by his deep desire to spread a better way of life and the teachings of his faith, and carried by his adventurous spirit, Livingstone undertook various major expeditions into Africa over the next 28 years. In so doing, he became the first European to encounter and

Previous spread: *Microlighting with Batoka Sky over the Victoria Falls.*
Above: *Statue of David Livingstone in Victoria Falls National Park.*

describe numerous major geographical features on the sub-continent to the outside world. These included the Kalahari Desert, Lake Ngami, Victoria Falls, the Upper Zambezi River, Lakes Tanganyika and Nyasa and the Rovuma and Congo rivers. He also achieved the first recorded trans-continental journey from west to east, and was influential in having the slave trade abolished. Along the way he opened trade routes and established various mission stations and education facilities, all the time fostering and spreading his sense of goodwill.

At the height of his fame during the 1850s, while back in Britain, Livingstone became something of a **heroic figure** and role model. He was feted everywhere and received numerous awards and accolades, took

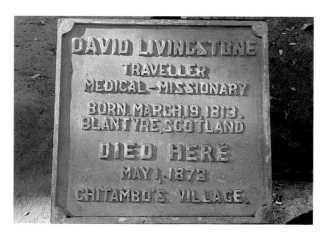

to the lecture circuit and published his first book, *Missionary Travels and Researches in South Africa*. But his travels and work were not without disappointment. After failing to navigate the length of the Zambezi River, the Zambezi Expedition was in some quarters labelled a failure, and he never did locate the source of the Nile River. While he was trusted and well respected by most of the African people he encountered, he did have disagreements with fellow travellers. On his last journey, disgruntled members who had abandoned the expedition reported him lost and dying in the interior; it was because of these reports that the New York Herald sent Henry Morton Stanley to find him. Reputedly as something of a publicity stunt, Stanley did eventually meet up with Livingstone at Ujiji, on the shores of Lake Tanganyika, when Stanley greeted him with the now famous words, **'Dr Livingstone, I presume?'**

Livingstone's death came a few years later when he succumbed to complications brought on by chronic malaria. After covering almost 48 000 kilometres on his journeys, he spent his last days being carried by porters before they decided he could go no further. They set up camp in the village of Ilala, a short distance from the shores of Lake Bangweulu, and in the early hours of the morning on 1 May 1873, Livingstone was found kneeling at his bedside, having died in prayer. In accordance with his wishes, his heart was buried under a tree outside his hut, and after drying and salting his body, it was carried by his loyal porters, Sussi and Chuma, to Bagamoyo on the coast of Tanzania, and shipped back to England. Livingstone was buried in Westminster Abbey on 18 April 1874.

LIVINGSTONE CHRONOLOGY

1813: Livingstone was born in Blantyre, Scotland.

1838: He moved to London and was accepted into the London Missionary Society.

1840–1844: He set sail for South Africa on his first expedition, where he began work at the Kuruman Mission, established by Dr Robert Moffat. Livingstone soon established his own mission at Mabotsa, near Kuruman in the Northern Cape. In 1844, he married Mary Moffat and they had four children.

1845–1849: From his mission station, Livingstone headed north through the Kalahari into (then) Bechuanaland (now Botswana). In 1849 he reached Lake Ngami, on the southern edge of the Okavango Delta.

1851–1852: On another trip, Livingstone reached the upper Zambezi River near the town of Sesheke, after crossing the Linyanti and Chobe Rivers. He later returned to Cape Town, putting his family aboard a ship for England. He left the Cape in June 1852, heading back to the Zambezi River.

1853–1856: Livingstone returned to the Linyanti and Chobe regions in 1853, before heading west to map a route to the Atlantic Coast, reaching Luanda in May 1854. After returning from the Atlantic via the Linyanti, Livingstone had his first encounter with slave traders and the slave caravans of the time. On 17 November 1855, he became the first European to describe the Victoria Falls, before heading eastwards in search of the Zambezi River mouth. Later, in December 1856, he returned to a hero's welcome in London.

1857: Livingstone received extensive recognition from the Royal Geographical Society, the American Geographical and Statistical Society, the Geographical Society of Vienna, the Geographical Society of Paris and the University of Oxford, among others. He was awarded medals and degrees and various other honours, and given the freedom of London, Glasgow and Edinburgh. Livingstone resigned from the London Missionary Society.

1858–1861: With his wife and brother, Livingstone returned to Africa in 1858 as the commander in charge of the government funded Zambezi Expedition. He began his next trip from the mouth of the Zambezi River and explored upstream as far as the Kebrabassa Rapids, now the site of the Cahora Bassa Dam. He then headed north along the Shire River and reached Lake Nyasa in 1859, where he spent a number of years.

1862–1864: Livingstone's wife Mary died of dysentery in 1863, before he again returned to Britain in 1864, via Zanzibar, after the Zambezi Expedition was called off by the British government.

1865–1870: As part of his anti-slavery campaign and in search of the source of the Nile River, he embarked on his final expedition. He sailed via Bombay and reached Stone Town in Zanzibar in 1866. Months later he headed for the mainland and explored the central regions, following the Rovuma River. He reached the shores of Lake Tanganyika in 1868, via Lake Bangweulu. In 1870, he reached the Congo River. During this period Livingstone was taken ill and lost touch with the outside world.

1871: Henry Morton Stanley, the American correspondent from the New York Herald, met up with Livingstone in Ujiji on 23 October, on the shores of Lake Tanganyika. The two spent some time exploring the lake shores together.

1873: On 1 May, Livingstone died in northern Zambia while in prayer, not far from the shores of Lake Bangweulu.

1874: His body was laid to rest in Westminster Abbey, London.

Opposite: *This plaque is situated on the edge of Lake Bangweulu.* **Below:** *Trucks wait their turn to cross the Chobe River on the Kazangula Ferry.*

Land reform in Zimbabwe

While current political and socio-economic issues would generally be beyond the scope of this book, the significance of what has occurred in Zimbabwe over the past years requires commentary. It has particular relevance because conditions in the country may influence the choices made by travellers.

In essence, **the tragedy** that has occurred in Zimbabwe is the result of attempts to resolve past injustices in a woefully short-sighted and chaotic manner. In the process, a legitimate and urgent need for a national land reform programme was hijacked for the sake of short-term political gain. Poor planning and disordered execution, fuelled by political bickering and expediency, and a blatant disregard for the rule of law, resulted in the near collapse of a once sound country. The impact: during the period 2001 to 2006, Zimbabwe had the fastest shrinking non-war economy in the world; over 60 per cent of the population was classified as living in abject poverty; both local and foreign investment dried up totally, and millions of its citizens left.

In the two decades prior to 2000, Zimbabwe was in most quarters regarded as a stable, peaceful and relatively successful democratic country. Annual growth rates averaged around 3,5 per cent, the country was one of the largest food producers on the sub-continent, there was a thriving tourism industry and the country had a well-developed infrastructure. Its major concern was one fairly typical of most recently independent ex-colonial countries in Africa: high levels of income inequality, in this case exacerbated by a massively skewed land ownership regime where the small white minority owned the vast majority of the most productive agricultural land. While these almost 5 000 farms contributed more than 40 per cent of Zimbabwe's national exports and were the largest employer, millions of black people were left to eke out a living in overcrowded and unproductive communal lands. Clearly, reform involving the **redistribution of productive land** was urgently needed.

Historically, land had been a source of conflict ever since the first European and Dutch settlers arrived. In 1965, Ian Smith, leader of the white minority regime that governed Rhodesia, announced a unilateral declaration of independence (UDI) from the United Kingdom. Based on a racist policy of separate development that excluded the black majority from mainstream political decision making, this was seen by the world as a hostile move and was not recognised by the United Nations. It was a move that in effect 'legally' placed the vast majority of good agricultural land in the hands of the white minority and left the black majority to share what was known as Tribal Trust Lands. UDI heralded the formation of various black opposition movements and the beginning of a low-intensity bush war for full independence. Fifteen years later, when the various parties signed the **Lancaster House Agreement** (LHA), brokered by the British, the pact brought an end to the war and paved the way for the country's first free elections. These were won by the Zimbabwe African National Union (ZANU) and, with Robert Mugabe as the first Prime Minister, the country gained full independence on 18 April 1980.

At the time, all parties involved in the LHA accepted that land reform was a priority and to this end provisions were made, both financial and political, to redress the situation. But the same agreement also contained various clauses guaranteeing the economic and political status of the white population for a period of ten years. Amongst these was a provision protecting land ownership rights and a stipulation that any land claims by government would be settled at market prices on a 'willing buyer, willing seller' principle.

Little headway was made with land reform in the first decade after independence until the special clauses pertaining to the white population expired in 1990. Various new land acts and amendments to property rights followed (National Land Policy 1990 and Land Acquisition Act 1992). These included the introduction of property taxes to help fund land purchases. Despite these changes and the government having listed 1 471 farms for acquisition, according to an in-depth report by Human Rights Watch (www.hrw.org), by 1997 the government had resettled '71 000 families (against a target of 160 000) on almost 3.5 million hectares of land (against a target of nine million). Only 19 per cent of this was classed as prime land; the rest was either marginal or unsuitable for grazing or cultivation.

A Zimbabwean family heads into town on market day.

About 400 black elite farmers were leasing 400 000 hectares of state land, and about 350 black people had bought their farms.'

There were a number of reasons for government **failing to deliver** on their land reform promises: bureaucratic inefficiency and corruption, government budgetary constraints, intransigence on the part of the commercial farmers, and a lack of urgency from all parties had all been major contributory factors. There were also disputes over donor funding. Although an amount of 44 million pounds had been donated, mostly by the British government, the Zimbabwean government viewed this as insufficient, claiming that, as the ex-colonial power, Britain had an obligation to fund land purchases and should be contributing more. The British in turn held back further funding, pointing out as reasons their concerns about transparency and cronyism, with political figures and ZANU party insiders gaining access to land rather than the landless poor.

While these land issues were coming to a head during the late 1990s, there were other political problems that were playing themselves out. Soldiers who had fought in the various liberation movements had formed a **'War Veterans'** association and they were pressurising government for financial payouts and land compensation for their efforts in securing independence. Bowing to the increasingly strident lobbying, Mugabe personally intervened and approved a once off Z$50 000 payment and Z$2 000 monthly allowance for each veteran, with promises of land to follow. In what was possibly the most ill-considered and costly move at the time, the Zimbabwe government then committed over 11 000 troops to the Democratic Republic of Congo, where rebel forces were at war with the incumbent government. These two initiatives placed immense strain on the government's finances, adding further pressures to an already deteriorating local economy. The country had substantial foreign loans to service and along with droughts and falling export earnings, inflationary pressures and a fast-declining currency were the result. Zimbabwe was not in good shape.

This wretched state of affairs brought the people of Zimbabwe into the streets, with widespread mass action in the form of strikes and protests taking place. For the first time, the trade unions of the country had shown their strength, and it was considerable. These strikes were the precursor to the formation of the Movement for Democratic Change (MDC), a political party formed by various interest groups to challenge Mugabe at future elections. The MDC also attracted widespread support and funding from the white community and outlined a more promising and urgent land reform programme than that being carried out by the government.

In the meanwhile, in an effort to speed up the land reform programme, a major land conference attended by all parties, including donors, was held in Harare in September 1998. Despite these efforts, the response for new pledges from donors was poor, and there was a noticeable deterioration in relations between Zimbabwean and British officials, with the British firmly of the opinion that land previously acquired by government should be appropriately distributed before further funding was made. By late 1999, Human Rights Watch estimated that '11 million hectares of the richest land were still in the hands of about 4 500 commercial farmers, the great majority of them white.' Against this, the communal lands were now carrying even greater population densities and were for the most part over-utilised.

In February 2000, Mugabe held a national referendum in the hope that draft changes to the constitution would be approved, including sweeping new powers for the executive branch of government and the ability to acquire land without compensation. With its support base growing rapidly, the **opposition MDC** won the day, garnering 53 per cent of the vote, and with a general election due in June 2000, it was apparent that for the first time since 1980, the government was in real danger of losing its grip on power.

It was against this background that Mugabe played his trump card in an effort to stay in power: he introduced a 'fast track' land reform programme. Although officially launched only in July 2000, with the war veterans at the helm and tacit assistance from every branch of the government, including the army and police, the **'fast track' programme** had in fact begun months earlier. Mugabe won the election, although not without cries of election fraud, and only by the slimmest of margins. Success at the polls gave the 'fast track' programme substantial impetus as farms were literally invaded, and encouraged Mugabe to push the constitutional changes rejected in the earlier referendum through parliament. Widespread legal challenges by farmers followed and, despite being upheld by the courts, these were ignored as judges were simply removed from their posts and changes to the law that favoured the government were made.

By January 2002, the government had listed approximately 4 000 farms covering over nine million hectares for acquisition. These were denoted as either model A1, for landless people and war veterans to undertake subsistence farming, or model A2, for small- to medium-scale commercial farmers. Despite attempts at formalising the process, by the end of the year the land reform programme had become a frontier-like **land grab**. Emboldened by a breakdown in the rule of law and spurred on by government officials, the new claimants drove farmers off their farms, often after violent confrontations. With reports of disorder and violence spreading around the world, the country's economy was well and truly in a process of 'meltdown'. The currency exchange rate was in freefall, the once robust agricultural sector had been all but destroyed and the country was experiencing food shortages and a chronic fuel crisis. Local and foreign investment had ceased. Government was reneging on commitments given at various local and international conferences, land was being used as a political tool, political violence against MDC leaders and supporters was widespread, and millions had lost their jobs and homes.

To date, over 4 500 farms, covering almost 11 million hectares of land, have been claimed by the government, leaving fewer than 500 commercially driven farming units in operation in Zimbabwe. Exact statistics are sketchy, but it is thought that somewhere between 200 000 and 300 000 families have been resettled. Most analysts agree that until Mugabe goes, Zimbabwe is unlikely to win sufficient assistance to turn its fortunes around.

A new landowner prepares her first cotton crop for the market.

The guard at the gate of the local camp site in Victoria Falls.

19

be ENTICED

Previous spread: *During peak periods, water flows over the Victoria Falls at more than 500 million litres per minute.*

Above: *The waterfall spray rises almost 400 metres into the air and can be seen from up to 30 kilometres away.*

Opposite: *Boogie boarding at rapid 5.*

A visit to Victoria Falls, Livingstone and Chobe is literally a journey to the **geographical heart** of Southern Africa. It places one at the epicentre of a greater region that covers so many other fascinating and worthwhile destinations. Most are within close proximity and reaching them, whether under your own steam, by boat or by charter flight, will not require any major logistical planning or itinerary disruptions.

Zimbabwe and Zambia

THE SMOKE THAT THUNDERS
One of the Seven Natural Wonders of the World, the cascading waters, spray showers and rainbows of Victoria Falls are a truly incredible spectacle. It is equally impressive from the Zimbabwean or the Zambian sides, particularly so during the peak flow in March and April, and over a full moon when the lunar rainbow adds an aura of the surreal.

ADRENALINE OPTIONS
Swallow your butterflies – take to the water, the air or the cables and binge on the thrill of a variety of adrenaline activities second to none. Operators in Victoria Falls and Livingstone will keep you occupied for as long as your heart and nerve can hold out.

THE VICTORIA FALLS HOTEL
On the Zimbabwean side, the hotel is the region's most famous landmark after the Falls. Colonial and grand, it has the best hotel views of the gorge and railway bridge. Stay here if you can. Otherwise, book for an evening buffet dinner or try the sumptuous afternoon tea at the very least.

HWANGE
Zimbabwe's premier national park should be on any itinerary to the region. Expansive, private and with the densest wildlife concentrations, the concessions of Linkwasha and Makololo in the south are the places to be. While the dry winter months offer the best game viewing, the ever-changing colours and moods of massive summer-storm skies make this season no less appealing.

MATETSI
With an option of two luxurious safari camps, one verging on the banks of the Zambezi River, the other set back in the verdant grass plains, the Matetsi Private Game Reserve offers a most rewarding safari experience. Only 40 kilometres out from Victoria Falls, it is the perfect choice for those visitors to Zimbabwe who do not have the waterfall as their priority.

Opposite, top:
*Doing the 'flying fox'
with Wild Horizons on
the Victoria Falls town
side of the gorge.*
Opposite, bottom:
*Canoeing upstream
of the waterfall is
a worthwhile day
excursion.*
Left: *The viewing deck
of Taita Falcon Lodge
above rapid 17.*

TAITA FALCON LODGE

As far as settings go, there is nothing more outrageously spectacular along the Zambezi than this lodge. Perched on the very edge of the gorge on the Zambian side, almost 200 metres up and overlooking the swirling waters of rapids 16 and 17, Taita Falcon offers the region's most picture perfect views.

SINDABEZI ISLAND

Rustic comfort, romance and tranquillity are the hallmarks of this charming Zambian river hideaway. Tucked away on a small wooded island in the swirls of the Zambezi River, Sindabezi is the perfect pick for small groups and families in search of that private getaway.

THE RIVER CLUB

Situated on a broad, sweeping Zambezi River bend, above Victoria Falls, the River Club is Livingstone's premier luxury option – and if the colonial feel is to your liking, the Edwardian styling, complete with croquet lawns, will be the clincher.

KAFUE NATIONAL PARK

After decades of neglect, Zambia's largest and most diverse national park is on the comeback. Exciting camp openings and infrastructural developments are great news for the region and just the impetus Kafue needs to regain its place as one of the continent's leading wildlife destinations.

THE KUOMBOKA CEREMONY

This is a ceremony carried out in the most venerable of ways, and with an immense sense of pride and honour for the traditions of the Lozi people and their king. The spectacle is enhanced by the extremely tangible and obvious levels of excitement and enjoyment experienced by thousands and thousands of citizens of Barotseland, who willingly flock from all parts of the province to participate in some way.

Below: *A hippopotamus, a night-time visitor on Sindabezi Island.*
Opposite: *Visit the Falls Craft Village for insights into local cultures and customs.*

Botswana

CHOBE CHILWERO

Chobe National Park in Botswana is world renowned for its prolific elephant population, particularly in the drier winter months, when tens of thousands of these massive animals congregate. Viewed from a game drive vehicle or on a sunset cruise, this spectacle is best experienced based at Chobe Chilwero, a luxurious lodge located away from the crush.

IMPALILA ISLAND LODGE

Nowhere is the well-used marketing catch phrase of 'location, location and location' more apt than in reference to this delightful luxury island lodge. Situated closest to the point where the four countries of the region meet – Botswana, Namibia, Zimbabwe and Zambia – Impalila's location is perfect for geography buffs and those in search of first-rate fly fishing and birding, along with access to Chobe National Park.

Viewing elephant along the Chobe River.

Wild dog, an endangered species, can still be seen in Chobe National Park.

from RIVERS
to ROPES & RAFTING

Situated centrally within the Southern African region, the three countries of Botswana, Zimbabwe and Zambia **share common boundaries** and form a bloc that integrates their relatively well-developed infrastructures. This not only serves them well, but also acts as a conduit for transport and trade to Central and East Africa. In more recent history, the region has enjoyed relative peace, and despite their currently differing fortunes, these countries are globally well known and sought after as tourist destinations.

Previous spread: *The African Princess, Livingstone's premier river cruise boat.*
Below: *The edge of the Victoria Falls on the Zambian side.*
Opposite: *Great Zimbabwe, situated south of Masvingo, is a World Heritage site.*

Zimbabwe

Zimbabwe has received substantial, global press coverage over the past few years, but unfortunately this has mostly been a chronicle of the sad and swift collapse of this country's economy and much of its social and political fabric. Brought on primarily by a 'fast track' land reform programme gone wrong, a **once stable** middle income economy and one of the continent's major food producers has almost halved its annual GDP of US$8.4 billion in 1997 to approximately US$4.4 billion in 2005. In the calamitous process, export earnings have slumped by 60 per cent, employment by 40 per cent and agricultural output, the backbone of the economy, by 68 per cent. Other knock-on effects have included a collapsing currency; spiralling hyperinflation; chronic food and fuel shortages; a substantial reduction in foreign aid, lending and investment; and increasing **political tensions** amongst the various sectors of the population. As a consequence, millions of its citizens have fled for greener pastures.

Prior to independence in 1980, the country's white minority had already established a substantial and well-developed agricultural sector and a solid infrastructural foundation. However, because of the then government's segregationist political policies, the general economy was held back by sanctions and exclusions placed by the world community. It was only during the first 15 years or so after independence that the country achieved most of its growth and stature as it became integrated into the wider African and global environment. By the mid-1990s, Zimbabwe's fortunes seemed sound. The remaining colonial hangover that still had to be dealt with was the immensely **skewed land ownership** situation that saw the majority of productive land in the hands of the white minority. Few people disagreed that the situation needed redress, but even fewer would have opted for the path chosen by Robert Mugabe and his ZANU PF government (see 'Land Reform in Zimbabwe' on page 14).

While the crisis still continues, there is much hope that change will come, sooner rather than later, and once the present leader and his worst cohorts have been moved on, Zimbabwe will begin its rehabilitation. It will require a massive effort by those who have stayed, but they will no doubt be supported by tens of thousands of returning citizens, many of whom represent the intellectual and skilled capital of the country; and by the international community.

BRIEF HISTORY OF ZIMBABWE

10 000 BC: Zimbabwe's earliest inhabitants were the semi-nomadic, hunter-gatherer San people. There are numerous rock art sites, found throughout Zimbabwe.

AD 100: The first settlers into the region were Bantu-speaking peoples who began arriving approximately 2 000 years ago, bringing livestock and the practices of ironwork and cultivating crops with them.

500–900: The earliest descendants of the Shona people, the largest group in present-day Zimbabwe, were settled by the ninth century. These pastoralist people brought stonework, mining techniques and pottery with them, all activities that resulted in wealth creation and political organisation.

1000–1450: The kingdom of Mwene Mutapa (referred to as Monomotapa in colonial history books) was established by a dynasty descended from the Gokomere people. Its centre was the amazing, stone-structured city of Great Zimbabwe, located outside the present-day town of Masvingo. At its most powerful, from the eleventh to the thirteenth centuries, the kingdom covered most of Zimbabwe and southern Zambia, stretching eastwards to the Mozambique coast, and southwards into parts of South Africa. Its wealth was based on iron smelting, gold and copper mining, ivory and agriculture.

1500–1600: Most of the kingdom's earlier trade engaged the Swahili, Arabs and Persians, but during the 1500s, the Portuguese began trading. They also attacked the kingdom in an attempt to gain control of the gold mines, and although defeated, they established a more influential presence in the region. It was also during this period that other dynasties and chieftainships established themselves.

1600–1800: The decline of Mwene Mutapa set in during the sixteenth century, through a combination of falling gold prices, overgrazing in the area and conquest by the Portuguese. At the same time, the Rozwi Empire emerged, a kingdom formed by splinter groups from Mwene Mutapa. They were at their most influential from the mid-1600s until the late 1700s. In 1693, they defeated the Portuguese in battle.

1800–1850: By the mid-1800s, the demise of the Rozwi Empire coincided with the period known in African history as the Difaquane. Brought about by overpopulation and drought, this was a period in the early 1800s that saw the expansion of the Zulu kingdom from the south. Led by the military leader Shaka, this resulted in many wars that forced the migration and resettlement of various groups northwards. It was also during this period that the first European explorers, traders and missionaries began settling in Zimbabwe.

1840: Mzilikazi, the first leader of the present-day Ndebele people, settled in the region around Bulawayo, in Matabeleland. A Zulu by birth, he fled the Zulu kingdom with his extended family in 1823 after a quarrel with Shaka, passing through Mozambique and South Africa on his way northwards. The Ndebele ruled over most of western Zimbabwe, displacing numerous Shona-speaking groups as their kingdom expanded. Their wealth was based on cattle.

1855: David Livingstone reached the Zambezi River and became the first European to set eyes on the Victoria Falls.

1868–1890: Mzilikazi died in 1868 and was succeded by his son, Lobengula, who became king in 1870. Meanwhile, in 1865, gold had been discovered in the region, which brought an influx of prospectors and money men, including Cecil John Rhodes and his British South Africa Company. This was also the period when the scramble for Africa by European powers was at its peak.

1890: The Pioneer Column of Cecil John Rhodes arrived in Fort Salisbury, present-day Harare. He named the city after the third Marquess of Salisbury, the then British Prime Minister. Rhodes set about establishing his business, political and infrastructural interests through his British South Africa Company, granted a Royal Charter by Queen Victoria.

1893: Under Leander Starr Jameson, a British troop defeated Lobengula, bringing to an end the rule of the Ndebele and with it, the promise of good agricultural land and mining rights, heralding an influx of colonial settlers.

1895: The territory became informally known as Rhodesia, taking its name from Cecil John Rhodes.

1897: The British managed to overcome a rebellion of combined Ndebele and Shona forces, aimed at trying to rid the country of white settler rule.

1911: The country became officially known as Southern Rhodesia.

This drawing, depicting the meeting of David Livingstone and Henry Morton Stanley, hangs in the foyer of The Stanley and Livingstone hotel outside Victoria Falls town.

1923–1930: In September 1923, the role of the British South Africa Company ended when the white settlers vote for self-governing colony status in a referendum. In 1930, the colony passed the Land Appointment Act, establishing 'native reserves' and prohibiting Africans from buying land.

1953: The colonies of Southern Rhodesia, Northern Rhodesia (Zambia) and Nyasaland (Malawi) were brought together as the Central African Federation. The federation was dissolved in 1963, prior to the independence of Zambia and Malawi.

1962–1963: After various other political parties had been banned, Josuah Nkomo formed the Zimbabwe African Peoples Union (ZAPU). In 1963, the Rev. Ndabaningi Sithole led a breakaway group from ZAPU and formed the Zimbabwe African National Union (ZANU) with Robert Mugabe. The party was based on Shona ethnicity.

1965: Under the leadership of Ian Smith, the right-wing Rhodesian Front unilaterally declared independence (known as UDI) from the British government and the country became known as Rhodesia. This step went unrecognised by any other country, or the United Nations.

1966: Rhodesia withdrew from the Commonwealth and UDI served to bring the two leading liberation movements, ZANU and ZAPU together as the Patriotic Front (PF). The PF began its armed struggle for independence against the Rhodesian government. In 1968, the United Nations applied economic and political sanctions against the country.

1973: Robert Mugabe completed his ten-year prison term for political activity and became the leader of ZANU. He moved to Mozambique, while Joshua Nkoma and ZAPU were based in Zambia.

1975: In April, peace talks between the Rhodesian government, led by Prime Minister Ian Smith, and various nationalist leaders, led by Bishop Abel Muzorewa, were held aboard a carriage parked in the middle of Victoria Falls Bridge. The talks failed as Ian Smith refused to grant immunity from prosecution to returning liberation movement leaders.

1978–79: International pressure and an inability to win the armed conflict forced the Rhodesian government to the negotiating table. In 1979, they signed an internal agreement with the United African National Council and various other small moderate African parties, and a general election was held. Under the leadership of Bishop Abel Muzorewa, the country was known as Zimbabwe-Rhodesia until April 1980. Because it did not include the major liberation movements, the internal agreement was not recognised outside of the country. Shortly after the internal agreement, the Commonwealth called for further talks including the two major liberation parties. The Lancaster House Agreement was signed in December 1979, heralding the end of the armed struggle and paving the way for a new constitution and the country's first free and fair elections.

1980: On 18 April, Zimbabwe gained full independence, with Robert Mugabe, returned from exile in January of the same year, as the country's first freely elected leader.

1982–1985: Robert Mugabe sacked Nkomo from the cabinet. After skirmishes with pro-Nkomo ex-guerillas, Mugabe unleashed the Fifth Brigade, a North Korean trained unit of the Zimbabwean army, against the people of Matabeleland. In the conflict, almost 20 000 people were killed, most buried in mass graves south of Bulawayo.

1987: Robert Mugabe (ZANU) and Josuah Nkomo (ZAPU) reconciled their differences, merging their two parties into a single party known as ZANU-PF.

1998: Zimbabwe underwent an economic crisis resulting in widespread strikes and mass action. These were a precursor to the formation of the opposition Movement for Democratic Change (MDC), an alliance of trade union and opposition groups.

2000: Land invasions of white-owned farms began. Mugabe was defeated by the MDC in a referendum on changes to the constitution, but narrowly won a general election held in June.

2001–2004: The country slipped into near chaos as land invasions continued and the economy collapsed amid currency, food and fuel shortages, and European Union sanctions. Mugabe clamped down on the media, judiciary and all opposition parties.

2005: In March, the ruling party won parliamentary elections amid widespread reports of election fraud, and in November won a majority of seats in the newly created Senate.

Factfile – Zimbabwe

(Note: Because of the collapse of Zimbabwe's economy, statistics since 2000 are difficult to verify.)

Area	390 784 square kilometres
Population	12.94 million (2004 estimate)
Population density	33.1 people per square kilometre
Population growth rate	1.4%
Urban population	35%
Capital city	Harare
Principal cities and towns	Bulawayo, Gweru, Mutare, Kwekwe
National protected areas	7.9%
Other wildlife management	7.0%
Independence	1980
National Day	18 April
Official language	English
Currency	Zimbabwe Dollar (Z$)
Economic growth rate	–6.5% (2005)
Annual GDP	US$4.4 billion
Gross National Income (GNI)	US$480 per capita (2004)
Poverty	51.6% live on US$1 per day (2004)
Human Development Index	Ranked 147th out of 177 states

- Zimbabwe was a former British colony known as Southern Rhodesia, and from 1965, as Rhodesia.
- At independence, a new constitution was drawn up for the Republic of Zimbabwe that included a Declaration of Rights.
- The President is Head of State, head of the government and Commander of the Armed Forces. The President is elected for a six-year term by majority vote at national elections. The number of terms is unlimited. Parliament consists of two chambers. The National Assembly has 150 seats, 120 of which are elected by majority vote in elections held every five years. The remaining seats are made up of 10 chiefs, 8 provincial governors and 12 members nominated by the President. The second chamber, the Senate, came into being during 2005. It consists of 65 seats, of which 50 are elected, with the balance going to traditional chiefs and presidential appointees.
- Since independence, the government has pushed through 17 sets of changes to the constitution.

- Until the land invasions of white-owned farms in early 2000, agriculture was the backbone of Zimbabwe's economy. Wide scale commercial farming made the country one of Africa's leading food producers. The sector contributed approximately 20 per cent of GDP, accounted for over 40 per cent of foreign exchange earnings and provided employment for almost 75 per cent of the working population. Tobacco was the leading export crop and the country was a major beef exporter. Other sectors include seed maize, sugar cane, wheat, cotton, vegetables, fruit, tea, coffee and cut flowers.
- Historically, the country has had a well-diversified manufacturing sector contributing approximately 25 per cent of GDP, 20 per cent of exports and employing 15 per cent of the workforce. The main industries have been food and beverage processing, chemicals, textiles and light engineering. This sector has also been adversely affected by political and economic problems, with little new investment taking place.
- Prior to the onset of Zimbabwe's woes, tourism was the fastest growing sector in the economy, with an average 20 per cent increase annually since the late 1980s. It was the third largest foreign exchange earner, contributed approximately 6 per cent to GDP and employing over 200 000 people. Visitor numbers fell from 1.4 million in 1999 to approximately 250 000 in 2005, with a resulting loss of tens of thousands of jobs. The 2005/2006 season saw the first signs of recovery in this sector.
- The mining sector contributes 30 per cent of foreign exchange earnings. The principal minerals are gold, chrome, nickel, coal, iron ore and the platinum group metals.
- The country's legal system is a mix of Roman Dutch law, English common law and customary law. Numerous regional and Magistrates Courts operate below the High Court, and the Supreme Court is the final court of appeal. At a local level, Customary Courts are presided over by chiefs and headmen and deal with limited matters, involving customary village disputes.
- Primary school education is free and compulsory and begins at six years of age, lasting for seven

years. Many of the country's high schools have an extremely good reputation, drawing pupils from countries within the sub-continent. Zimbabwe has two state universities and two private universities, and numerous technical and teacher training colleges. Primary school enrolment is 90 per cent and adult literacy is 93 per cent.

- The country is a member of the African Union, the United Nations and the Southern African Development Community (SADC).

- The Zimbabwean flag consists of a series of horizontal stripes. Green represents the country's natural resources, yellow the mineral wealth, red the blood of those who died in the liberation struggle and black stands for the people. These colours are also the official ruling party colours, and those of Pan-African movements. The white triangle to the side represents peace, the red star is a symbol of internationalism and the Zimbabwe bird over the star is the national emblem of Zimbabwe.

A market scene at Victoria Falls.

Zambia

While still listed as one of Africa's **least developed** countries, Zambia's political and economic fortunes have improved somewhat since 1991. Until then, 27 years of heavy socialism under the authoritarian rule of Kenneth Kaunda, the country's first and only President, had not brought significant political and economic development. During his tenure, the size of the country's economy was substantially reduced from its British colonial inheritance in 1964. The country was in effect a repressive, one-party state. Kaunda's only real success, ironically based on a vision of 'humanism', was to forge a united Zambian identity from a nation of people with seventy-odd different language groups. Growing civil unrest ended Kaunda's rule and a new constitution, based on a **multiparty democracy**, dawned with much promise for the country and its citizens.

The new government, under the leadership of Frederick Chiluba, soon set about transforming the country's institutions. Since then, the electoral system has, for the most part, delivered and the judiciary and press are now regarded as being reasonably free and fair, but economic progress has been less successful. The country has always had a single-commodity economy based on copper, and its general fortunes have surged and dipped in line with the movements of the global copper price. A severe price slump during the 1970s and 1980s resulted in substantially reduced foreign earnings. Along with fears of total nationalisation of the industry, capital investment dwindled. As a result, the government turned to international lenders and foreign aid for relief. By the early 1990s, cumulative debt, along with poor fiscal management, had become a major economic burden that almost crippled the country. During this period, for example, debt repayments were double the amounts allocated to education and health budgets.

While there has since been some international debt relief, (US$3.9 billion was written off in 2005), the legacy of outstanding amounts remains onerous, and the relief has come with stringent 'structural adjustment programmes' placed by the likes of the World Bank and the International Monetary Fund (IMF), restricting social development. As a result, present spending on health, education and poverty alleviation remains at levels which are unable materially to improve the lives of the almost 65 per cent of Zambians, living on or below the poverty line. The challenge for future governments will be to step up the economic diversification process, away from its reliance on copper, and promote investment in sectors such as agriculture, tourism and export-orientated manufacturing. Along with these initiatives, corruption needs to be tackled and a heavy state bureaucracy reduced, both of which are deterrents to much-needed foreign investment.

Despite these huge economic and social challenges, the country has achieved much over the last decade in terms of infrastructural development. Lusaka, the capital city, and Livingstone, the **'tourism capital'** have undergone extensive face-lifts, and the major road network linking the principal cities and towns is in the process of a substantial upgrade. It is now almost two decades since the end of the Kaunda era and most Zambians agree the country they now know is better off than when they were under the rule of their first President.

BRIEF HISTORY OF ZAMBIA

70 000 BC: The earliest inhabitants of present-day Zambia were the hunter-gatherer San people. While evidence exists of early Stone Age tools, dating back at least 100 000 years, Zambia's most famous skull, that of 'Broken Hill Man', unearthed near Kabwe in 1921, dates to a more recent period of about 70 000 years ago. Descendants of modern man go back about 20 000 years to the Late Stone Age.

1000 BC–AD 200: The first immigrants to settle in the region were Negroid Bantu-speaking groups from West and Central Africa, introducing iron-age technologies, livestock and agricultural practices to the region.

700–1200: The archaeological site along the Zambezi River, known as Ingombe Ilede, dates to this period and indicates an Iron Age community of craftsmen and traders. Remains found included pottery, copper implements, glass beads and burial sites with gold ornaments. These Bantu people were most likely to have traded with Great Zimbabwe and Swahili traders from the east coast of the continent.

1400–1700: Immigrant groups established chieftaincies and small kingdoms across the country. Of the dominant ones, the Chewa settled in the east, the Lozi came from central Angola and established their kingdom in western Zambia, various Kavango groups settled in the west and southwest and the largest groups, the Bemba and Lunda, settled in the north. Mwata Yamvo, a Lunda empire, extended through the present-day Democratic Republic of Congo and into northern Zambia.

1700–1800: Portuguese and Swahili traders opened up Zambia, initially for the export of metals and ivory, but later for slaves. In exchange for slaves, often captured and held by other African groups, the slave traders brought textiles, gunpowder and jewellery.

1800–1840: The impact of the Difaquane resulted in Nguni-based groups from the south moving northwards. These included the Kololo and various breakaway groups from the Zulu people, who were fleeing Shaka, the Zulu leader at the time. They settled in western and southern Zambia.

1851–1855: David Livingstone, the Scottish missionary, entered Zambia for the first time at Sesheke and established a mission station. In 1885 he became the first European to describe the Victoria Falls to the outside world.

1873: David Livingstone died on the shores of Lake Bangweulu.

1890: The Lozi king, Paramount Chief Lewanika, signed a mineral concession with Cecil John Rhodes's British South Africa Company (BSAC). This agreement in essence passed control of large parts of western and central Zambia into the hands of the BSAC, which had been granted a Royal Charter by Queen Victoria in the same year. In exchange, the Lozi received protection against neighbouring warring groups.

1894–1899: The BSAC assumed full control of the region, named Northern Rhodesia, and in the process also took control of Bemba and Lunda land to the north.

1910–1911: The territory was officially separated from Southern Rhodesia and became formally known as Northern Rhodesia, with Livingstone as its capital.

1923–1924: The rule of Rhodes's BSAC came to an end with Northern Rhodesia officially becoming a British protectorate. White settlers were encouraged to acquire land and Africans were excluded from the legislative bodies set up by the British.

1935: Lusaka replaced Livingstone as the capital city.

1930–1955: Although the BSAC had begun commercial prospecting for copper in the early 1920s, it was only in the early 1930s that mining techniques had improved sufficiently to exploit these deposits. Four large mines opened, providing employment for a substantial number of Africans who flocked to what became known as the Copperbelt. Managed by colonials and white South Africans, working conditions were harsh, stirring the first signs of political aspirations amongst the local people. Labour unions were formed and strike action took place. In 1951, the North Rhodesian African National Congress, led by Harry Nkumbula, was formed.

1953: The colonies of Southern Rhodesia (Zimbabwe), Northern Rhodesia (Zambia) and Nyasaland (Malawi) were brought together as the Central African Federation (CAF). Vast amounts of money were siphoned off by Southern Rhodesia from the copper mines of Northern Rhodesia. The federation was dissolved in 1963, prior to the independence of Zambia and Malawi.

1958–1960: In the wake of anti-Federation sentiments amongst the black population, Kenneth Kaunda led a breakaway from Nkumbula's party and formed the Zambian African National Congress (ZANC) in October 1958. The party was banned and Kaunda was imprisoned for nine months. In 1959, a group of more militant members left the ZANC to form the United National Independence Party (UNIP). Kaunda was released in early 1960 and became President of UNIP.

1962–1963: After a campaign of civil disobedience, organised by Kaunda, the authorities allowed elections for local governments. A number of parties won seats and UNIP called for the dissolution of the Federation and the drawing up of a new constitution.

1964: Northern Rhodesia became the Republic of Zambia and gained full independence on 24 October, with Kaunda as the first, freely elected leader.

1965: With Zambia surrounded by neighbours still under white minority control, the country offered support to the liberation movements fighting in Angola, South-West Africa, Rhodesia, South Africa and Mozambique.

Left: *Lozi men wear traditional dress when they participate in the Kuomboka ceremony.*
Next page: *HIV/AIDS is a major concern in Botswana, Zimbabwe and Zambia.*

1972–1973: Kuanda pushed changes to the constitution through Parliament, making the country a one-party state, or as government described it, 'a one-party participatory democracy'. Other than the ruling party, all other political parties were banned. In 1973, Kaunda was elected to a third term as President.

1974–1980: Copper prices fell and with the government's harsh socialist policies failing, the country's fortunes waned. Amidst discontent within the country and his own party, Kaunda declared a State of Emergency in 1976. As the sole candidate, Kaunda won a fourth term in 1978 and, in 1980, various UNIP and opposition members were arrested for an attempted coup.

1981–1990: The country's economic and political conditions continued to deteriorate. Rising food prices, shortages and increasing unemployment heralded a decade of strikes and widespread civil unrest, and a draconian response from Kaunda as he arrested, jailed and banned opponents and organisations.

1990: The ongoing unrest took its toll on Kaunda and UNIP as they were forced to end their monopoly on power. Kaunda conceded to talks on a new constitution and the introduction of a multiparty democracy. The first major opposition party, the Movement for Multiparty Democracy (MMD) was formed from a mix of UNIP defectors, opposition politicians and trade unionists.

1991: In August, the country introduced a new constitution allowing for a multiparty democracy and a new electoral system. Elections were held in October and Frederick Chiluba, the MMD candidate, won a resounding 81 per cent of the vote. Thus began a major restructuring of Zambian political and economic institutions.

1993–1996: Amidst unrest, Chiluba declared a three-month State of Emergency in 1993, before a group of ministers, led by Levy Mwanawasa, formed a breakaway party in 1994. Chiluba was re-elected in general elections in 1996, after making changes to the constitution that prohibited Kaunda from running as a presidential candidate. UNIP, Kaunda's party, boycotted the parliamentary elections.

2001: Chiluba's attempt to change the constitution, allowing him to run for a third presidential term, was defeated. Levy Mwanawasa, the MMD candidate, won the election by a slim margin, with a low voter turnout. Various opposition parties contested the outcome.

2002: Ex-President Chiluba was stripped of immunity from prosecution and charged with numerous counts of fraud and corruption during his period in office.

2006: In strongly contested parliamentary elections, Mwanawasa won a second term.

Factfile – Zambia

Area	752 614 square kilometres
Population	11.48 million (2004)
Population density	15.2 people per square kilometre
Population growth rate	2.3%
Urban population	36%
Capital city	Lusaka
Principal cities and towns	Ndola, Kitwe, Kabwe, Chingola, Chipata, Livingstone
National protected areas	8.5% (19 national parks)
Game management areas	22% (36 areas)
Independence	1964
National Day	24 October
Official language	English
Currency	Zambian Kwacha
Economic growth rate	5.1%
Annual GDP	US$3.7 billion
Gross National Income (GNI)	US$450 per capita
Poverty	63.7% live on US$1 per day
Human Development Index	Ranked 166th out of 177 states

- Zambia was formerly known as Northern Rhodesia and was a British colony.
- The Republic of Zambia's constitution, as amended in 1991 and again in 1996, provides for a multiparty democracy, with legislative power vested in a single chamber of parliament. The National Assembly has 158 members, of which 150 are elected through national elections held every five years, with the remaining eight nominated by the President.
- The Head of State is the President, who is elected by popular vote at the same time as the national elections. The President's office is limited to two, five-year terms. The President appoints the Vice President and a Cabinet.
- A second body, the House of Chiefs, has 27 members acting as an advisory body to the President and National Assembly.
- Zambia has nine provinces, divided into 72 districts. Although the capital city of Lusaka carries the highest population, the densest concentration of people is in the Copperbelt in the north, along the border with Angola, where a string of towns together have a population of almost 1.5 million.
- The country is listed as a low-income, developing nation and has a high level of income inequality.
- Historically, the performance of Zambia's economy has been based on its mineral wealth. The country is the world's largest producer of cobalt (20 per cent of global production) and the largest producer of copper in Africa (the eleventh largest in the world). Together, these minerals account for approximately 75 per cent of export earnings and 10 per cent of GDP. Copper production has declined steadily from its peak in the 1970s when Zambia was the world's fourth-largest producer. Other minerals include zinc, lead, coal, gold and diamonds. The mining sector accounts for almost five per cent of the workforce.
- The agriculture sector is as important to the economy because it contributes over 20 per cent of GDP, and almost 80 per cent of the workforce is involved in this sector in some way. The chief staple crops are maize, cassava and sorghum and the main cash crops are sugar cane, groundnuts, tobacco, beans, cotton and vegetables. Cut flowers and vegetables are the fastest growing sectors. Because of the farm invasions in Zimbabwe, many farmers have resettled in Zambia, making this industry one of the fastest growing in the country.
- Manufacturing accounts for almost 30 per cent of GDP – the major sectors are food and beverage processing, cement, hydroelectric power, chemicals and textiles. Trade liberalisation and nationalisation policies forced on Zambia by the World Bank and IMF during the 1990s, had an unexpectedly negative effect on the economy, with the manufacturing sector being the worst affected. The textile industry, for example, lost 132 manufacturing units and 90 per cent of its workforce between 1991 and 2002.
- While the tourism sector remains relatively undeveloped, it holds great promise for growth in the economy.
- Zambia's legal system is based on a mix of English common law and customary law. The law is administered through a number of local courts and Magistrates Courts operating below the High Court. The Supreme Court is the highest court and acts as the final court of appeal. The judiciary is independent of the State.
- While primary school education is mandatory in Zambia, it is not enforceable by law. Enrolment is at seven years of age. Schooling is free for seven years. In 2004, 83 per cent of school-going children enrolled. The country has two universities and numerous colleges, including 14 teacher training colleges. Adult literacy stands at 68 per cent.
- The country is a member of the African Union, United Nations, the Non-Aligned Movement (NAM), the Southern African Development Community (SADC), and the Common Market for Eastern and Southern Africa (COMESA), which has its headquarters in Lusaka.
- Zambia's flag comprises three vertical stripes, red, black and orange, on the bottom right hand side on a green background. The red is symbolic of bloodshed while fighting for independence; black represents the people of Zambia and orange stands for the country's mineral wealth. The green background symbolises the country's natural resources. The flag also has a soaring eagle, Zambia's national bird, representing freedom.

A mural at the local junior school in Sesheke, Zambia.

Botswana

Botswana's history is one of immense success and by any yardstick, a remarkable one that has few parallels in Africa. Formerly the British protectorate of Bechuanaland, the country began to flourish after independence in 1966. As a multiparty democracy, the country's leaders and citizens have created a peaceful and progressive country with one of the continent's most **dynamic economies**.

Prior to 1966, the country was ranked as one of the world's poorest, with a GDP per capita below US$200 and no economy to speak of other than a fledgling beef industry that survived only because of European subsidies. Educational facilities were minimal, with less than two per cent of the population having completed primary school, only a few thousand pupils attending secondary school and less than 100 students enrolled on university courses, all of which were outside the country. No urban settlements were large enough or sufficiently developed even remotely to warrant city status. The country played no role in either regional or continental politics and almost unbelievably, there was only one 12 kilometre-long paved road in the country.

In 1967, and not even a full year after independence, Botswana received a major boost: substantial diamond deposits were discovered in the central and southern regions of the country. Over the last two decades, the economy has achieved the world's highest average annual growth rate, and today the GDP per capita is in excess of US$3 500 while the national coffers hold over US$6 billion in foreign reserves. Primary school enrolment is approaching 400 000 pupils, secondary school over 150 000 and the country has its own university with various satellite campuses, teaching over 20 000 students. There are now in excess of 7 000 kilometres of paved roads and the capital, Gaborone, is a thriving metropolitan area that is one of the continent's fastest growing cities. Part of the reward is that Botswana has since become a respected and stable member of various multilateral organisations, both local and international.

While the **discovery of diamonds** has undoubtedly been the major catalyst for economic growth, a number of other factors have contributed to the overall achievement. The historical settlement of Botswana occurred largely because of people fleeing conflicts elsewhere, and so generally speaking, the populace is peace loving, with no history of civil war or other serious internal conflict. Unlike much of Africa, Botswana was never fully colonised and so avoided a divisive struggle for independence. It is a relatively homogenous nation, with almost 60 per cent of the people belonging to one of the Tswana groups, nearly all speaking Setswana, the national language. As a result, there is a patriotic unity, with the vast majority viewing themselves first and foremost as citizens of the country before considering the ethnic group to which they belong.

Above all, Botswana has been blessed with **great leaders**, men and women who have guided the nation and its people with vision and commitment. There are many examples, both in Africa and globally, where countries blessed with a far greater supply of natural resources have not even remotely achieved what this country has. Prosperity has been brought about because of the wise manner in which the substantial diamond revenues have been handled.

This is not to say that the country is without its **future challenges**. Although the diamond-based economic boom has had far-reaching benefits, the local economy is small and cannot thrive if it remains dependent on this single commodity alone. Africa is littered with single product economies gone bust. To avoid this, secondary and tertiary economic activities need to be promoted, preferably those of an export-based nature, holding the most promise for employment and sustainable growth along with wildlife-based ecotourism, one of the fastest growing sectors. This very necessary diversification will also help deliver on what is probably going to be the country's most demanding responsibility: that of meeting the considerable expectations held by the younger generation. There are many of them and they are restless. Raised and educated on the proceeds of the diamond industry, they now want to participate in the country's good fortune. Like so much of Africa, a life based on tradition in a rural setting has lost much of its appeal. For the younger generation, a career and an improved standard of living with modern conveniences, preferably within an urban community, has instead become the ambition. And the country has not escaped the continent-wide HIV and AIDS scare. It is of major concern that most surveys indicate that over 30 per cent of the population is infected, giving the country one of the highest rates worldwide. Fortunately, political will and financial resources are available. The country has introduced the Vision 2016 campaign, aiming at an AIDS-free Botswana by that date.

In spite of these demands, there is much hope for the future of Botswana. Ian Khama, the current Vice President and son of Sir Seretse Khama, is expected to become the next President. He is seen as a bold and inspiring man who will be able to lead the nation into the next era.

Botswana has just under 100 000 telephone lines installed and over 12 000 Internet users.

BRIEF HISTORY OF BOTSWANA

20 000 BC: Although comprising only a small sector of the population today, the semi-nomadic hunter-gatherer San people, known locally as the Basarwa, inhabited the area originally and for many thousands of years; as did the related pastoralist Khoikhoi. They are collectively named the Khoisan.

AD 190–AD 450: Bantu-speaking settlers from the north began moving into surrounding territories, bringing with them an Iron Age farming culture, based on the raising of cattle and cultivation of grain crops.

AD 500: In the ensuing centuries, the tendency of different chiefs and their followers to leave the main tribe and settle in other areas resulted in the settlement patterns of the region's modern people. The first to arrive were the Zhizo, thought to be the ancestors of the Bakalanga. They were a non-Setswana-speaking group of Bantu who came from present-day Zimbabwe.

1000–1300: The Toutswe, who settled in the Palapaye region a few hundred years later, followed the Zhizo, as did the Mapungubwe, who settled in the Mahalapye region around 1300.

1400–1500: Most of Botswana's present-day inhabitants are Setswana-speaking, or Tswana. They are descended from the Sotho people who originated around the headwaters of the Limpopo River. During the middle of the last century, the first groups to arrive were the Bakgalagadi, who settled in the south and central regions. Later came the Babirwa, settling in the Bobonong area.

1600–1700: Three brothers split from their clan, forming the beginnings of three prominent Setswana-speaking groups of today. The Bakwena settled in the Molepolole area, the Bangwaketse in the Kanye district and the Bangwato around Serowe.

1750–1800: The Bangwato split with Chief Khama I, remaining in Serowe while his brother, Tawana, moved north to establish the Batawana clan around Lake Ngami and the southern fringes of the Okavango Delta. Other non-Setswana-speaking people arrived during the late 1700s, mostly from the north. The Bayei, Mbukushu and Basubiya splintered from the Balozi kingdom in present-day Zambia and settled in the northern regions along the Linyanti, Chobe and Okavango rivers.

1800–1835: As the ivory, cattle and slave trade spread inland from the Cape Colony and the coasts of Mozambique and Angola, the whole area experienced increasingly unsettled times. The Boer trekkers from the Transvaal were involved in various cattle and land wars with the local people and Zulu militancy, known as the period of the Difaquane, forced many more groups to move into this region in search of land and peace. The Barolong and Balete came from the south. The Bakgatla and Batlokwa came from the southeast during the early to mid-1800s.

1841: The Christian missionary influence began in the early 1800s, with Robert Moffat the first to arrive. David Livingstone followed in 1841, establishing the first school in the country.

1872–1880: By the late 1870s the Bangwato, the largest Tswana nation, had taken control of the Kwena under the chiefdom of Khama III, who ruled from 1872 to 1923.

1885: As a result of Boer expansionism, and to a lesser extent the continuing Ndebele incursions from the northwest, Botswana came under British protection in 1885. The Berlin Conference defined the boundaries of present-day Botswana and a British protectorate was formally declared over the area then known as Bechuanaland. The administrative capital was Mafeking, which was in the adjoining Cape Colony outside the territory's borders. At one stage the protectorate fell under the control of the Cape Colony.

1894–1895: In 1894, Cecil John Rhodes and his British South Africa Company (BSAC) motivated for the annexation of Bechuanaland. This hostile move prompted three Batswana chiefs, Sebele, Khama III and Bathoen I, to sail for Britain in 1895 to petition the government to keep their land under British protection. They were successful after the British public sided with them, but with one condition: the BSAC was entitled to build a railway line to what became known as Southern Rhodesia through their lands.

1896: Chief Sekgoma, head of the Batawana, ceded Ghanzi to the British Government to allow white settlement to take place. In return the British gave sovereignty of Ngamiland to the Batawana.

1900: The last of the country's present-day groups to settle were the Mbanderu and the Baherero, who fled the German occupation of present-day Namibia in the early 1900s and established their livestock-based lifestyle along the western and southern reaches of the Okavango.

1910: As promised by the British to the three Chiefs, Bechuanaland was excluded from the Union of South Africa, established in 1910.

1923: Khama III was one of the chiefs involved in the agreement resulting in a protectorate. Under his rule, peace and stability returned to the land and his people, the Bangwato, became a leading force in Bechuanaland. On his death in 1923, he was succeeded by his son, Sekgoma, who died only two years later. Sekgoma's eldest son, Seretse, was just a child and his older half-brother, Tshekedi, ruled in his place.

1948: During this period, Seretse travelled to England for schooling and his tertiary education, and it was there that he met and married Ruth Williams, a white woman, in 1948. The marriage split his people back home. Tshekedi was a strict traditionalist and particularly strongly opposed. Because of the dispute, the British banned both Seretse and Tshekedi from tribal lands.

1956: Seretse was eventually allowed to return with his wife in 1956 but only as a private citizen, as he had been persuaded to renounce his claim to the Bangwato chieftainship.

1961: Since 1952, Seretse's supporters had begun to organise themselves politically and after his return, he became a member of both the executive and legislative councils, formed in 1961 in terms of the new Bechuanaland constitution drawn up a year earlier.

1962: In 1962 Seretse Khama and Ketumile Masire formed the moderate Bechuanaland Democratic Party (now the Botswana Democratic Party, BDP).

1965–1966: The protectorate was granted internal self-government in 1965 and on 30 September 1966 the country gained full independence when the Republic of Botswana came into being, with Seretse Khama as its first President and Gaborone as the administrative capital. Seretse Khama received a British knighthood shortly thereafter.

1967–1974: Diamonds were discovered at Orapa, followed by later discoveries at Jwaneng and Lethlakane. This was the major factor in the country achieving economic growth and independence from South Africa, and from 1969 onwards Botswana began to play a significant role in international politics, as a non-racial liberal government.

1980: Sir Seretse Khama died in 1980 and was succeeded by his deputy, Quett Masire.

1998: Quett Masire retired as President and was succeeded by his former deputy, Festus Mogae. Ian Khama, the son of Sir Seretse Khama, was appointed Vice President.

2004: Mogae began a second term after his party won 52 per cent of the vote in elections held during October. The next elections were set for October 2009.

Factfile – Botswana

Area	581 730 square kilometres
Population	1.68 million (2004 estimate)
Population density	2.92 people per square kilometre
Population growth rate	2.4%
Urban population	49.4%
Capital city	Gaborone
Principal cities and towns	Francistown, Lobatse, Selebi-Phikwe, Molepolole, Maun and Serowe
National protected areas	17%
Wildlife management areas	22%
Independence	1966
National Day	30 September
Official language	English
National language	Setswana
Currency	Pula
Economic growth rate	6.2% (2005)
Annual GDP	US$10.1 billion
Gross National income (GNI)	US$8 370 per capita
Poverty	23.5% live on US$1 per day
Human Development Index	Ranked 128th out of 177 states

- The country's name is derived from the fact that almost 60 per cent of its inhabitants are Tswana. Botswana means 'the land of the Tswana'. The language is called Setswana and the citizens are known as Batswana.
- The Republic of Botswana is a multiparty democracy, with legislative power vested in a single chamber of parliament. This body, the National Assembly, has a total of 44 members, 40 of whom are elected directly by the voting population, in elections that are held every five years. The members of the National Assembly elect the remaining four members from a list submitted by the President. In addition, the Attorney General and the Speaker of the House sit in the National Assembly.
- Executive power lies with the President of Botswana, who appoints a Vice President and Cabinet. The presidency is limited to two five-year terms in office.
- The House of Chiefs is an advisory body acting as a support to the National Assembly, particularly on issues relating to the rural areas and traditional life. This body has 15 members, comprising the eight chiefs from the principal groups within Botswana, and six who are in turn elected by these members.
- The Index of Economic Freedom lists Botswana as Africa's freest economy. During the period 1990 to 2004, Botswana was listed as the world's fastest growing economy.
- The country is the world's largest producer of diamonds. In 2005, it produced 31 million carats, which was 35 per cent of the global production. This sector is the major component of Botswana's economy, contributing approximately 72 per cent of foreign earnings and approximately 35 per cent of GDP. Other metals and minerals include copper, nickel, coal, cobalt, soda ash and gold.

The Attorney General's Chambers in the city centre of Gaborone.

An electricity station outside Gaborone, Botswana's capital city.

- Industry comprises almost 20 per cent of GDP. Textiles, food and beverage processing, light engineering, and leather and related craft products are the major components.
- Agricultural production, primarily beef, comprised over 45 per cent of GDP at independence in 1966, but this has now fallen below four per cent. The sector is, however, still the largest employer, providing some source of income for almost 80 per cent of the population. The country receives favourable subsidies from the European Union for its beef, which is exported mainly to the United Kingdom, Norway, Denmark, Italy and Greece. The national herd consists of almost three million cattle.
- Tourism is the fastest-growing sector within the economy and the one that supports the less developed northern and western regions of the country. Although its contribution to GDP is still below 20 per cent, it is a large employer. As the second largest foreign exchange earner, it has been responsible for creating enormous knock-on benefits to the secondary economy. Tourism offers great potential for the country going forward.
- Land tenure falls into three broad categories. Communal or Tribal Land comprises 71 per cent of the country; State Land comprises 23 per cent, including all national parks and reserves;

and Freehold Land occupies six per cent, mostly in the east and around Gaborone, Francistown and Ghanzi. All citizens living in communal areas are entitled to land free of charge for residential, agricultural and commercial purposes.
- In general, population density increases from west to east, with almost 80 per cent of the population living in the eastern corridor, from Francistown to Gaborone and surrounding towns. While the average density is just over 2.6 persons per square kilometre, in parts of the central regions there are less than 0.5 persons per square kilometre, and as high as 450 persons per square kilometre in the cities and towns of the east and south.
- Education is free. Although strongly encouraged, it is not compulsory in Botswana. There are over 730 primary schools and 270 secondary schools that provide 12 years of education with the best teacher-pupil ratio in Africa. The country has over 50 colleges and technical education facilities for school-leavers, and one university. The illiteracy rate is approximately 21 per cent.
- The legal system is based on Roman Dutch law and customary law. The law is administered through a number of regional Magistrates Courts operating below the High Court and a Court of Appeal. Customary Courts are recognised, dealing with minor issues within rural communities. The judiciary is viewed as being fully independent of the State; the ultimate penalty is that of death by hanging.
- Botswana was a founder member of the SADC (the secretariat remains in Gaborone), and is a member of the United Nations, the African Union, the Commonwealth, the Non-Aligned Movement, the Southern African Customs Union and the World Trade Organisation.
- The national flag comprises a simple grid pattern in blue, black and white. Blue represents rain and water and this colour dominates the flag as a symbol of the prosperity this precious natural element brings to the country. The black and white stripes are symbolic of racial harmony amongst the various race groups. The zebra, which appears on the coat of arms, is the country's national animal. Botswana has no national bird or flower.

The peace and tranquillity of a mokoro ride in the Jao Concession.

a REGION of RIVERS

Bodies of water have a mystical magnetism like no other geographical landscape feature. While they generally speak of life and vitality, in the case of rivers, so much of the appeal is carried in the power of the flow and their ability to forge a meandering course. We are quite simply drawn to them and few regions in Africa can boast two such **alluring river systems**, the Zambezi and the Chobe, within such close proximity.

Previous spread: *An aerial view of the Zambezi River flowing into the Victoria Falls.* **Below:** *Evening sunlight on the Zambezi River.*

Victoria Falls known as "Musi-Oa-Tunya" or the smoke that thunders, constitutes of the most spectacular natural wonders of the world. At seventeen hundred metres the Victoria Falls is one of the world's largest sheets of water with an average of 540 on litres (143 Million gallons) of water cascading into the Zambezi gorge below per te. The holder of this voucher will witness the ultimate view of "Musi-Oa-Tunya" a 1500ft platform perched high above the spray of the falls with a birds eye view of ezi River carving it's way through the basalt rock on it's journey to the Indian n.

good omens). David Livingstone, the man responsible for bringing the Zambezi to the attention of the world beyond Africa, apparently once referred to it as 'this magnificent stream', but most who have experienced its beauty and power prefer to call it the 'mighty Zambezi'.

THE UPPER ZAMBEZI

Rising from a slight spring at about 1 500 metres above sea level, in the hilly countryside of the Mwinilunga District of far northwestern Zambia, the Zambezi first flows westwards for approximately 80 kilometres before crossing into Angola. It soon bends southwards and back into Zambia, where it crosses flatter ground. It is in these upper lands that it gathers size and volume as countless tributaries feed their muddy waters into the system. By now a relentless force, it spreads out across the swampy wetlands and fertile floodplains of the Barotse Plain in western Zambia, before gathering into a wide body of water that borders Namibia's Caprivi Strip. Ever so briefly, it nicks Botswana where the Chobe River, the region's other major system, spills into the Zambezi at Kasane. It is here amongst the grass-lined waterways, in a region known to the locals as Four Corners, that the borders of four countries, Zambia, Zimbabwe, Botswana and Namibia, meet.

now the river has reached the basalt stratum that es the region and immediately after passing the ossing point at Kazangula, between Botswana ambia, it becomes the divide between Zambia mbabwe for almost 500 kilometres. Widening in to over 1.2 kilometres, it flows for approximately ometres more before plunging over the Victoria ee below), the river's most spectacular feature and vide between the Upper and Middle Zambezi.

MIDDLE ZAMBEZI

iately below the waterfall, the river zigzags its way h the narrow and steep-sided basalt walls of the a Gorge. At any time of the year it is impressive, ring peak flood times it moves as a raging torrent. essions of rapids follow and then, flanked by pments and somewhat wider now, the Zambezi aches its first man-made impediment, Lake Kariba, st 120 kilometres below the waterfall.

Below Kariba, the river flattens and widens again as it passes Mana Pools National Park and some of the most scenic stretches on its entire course. As it approaches Mozambique, it is given impetus from the waters of the Kafue River, the system's largest tributary, and then the Luangwa River, before entering its second man-made lake, Cahora Bassa, in the Tete Province of central western Mozambique. Almost 950 kilometres from the Victoria Falls, the dam wall is the divide between the Middle and Lower Zambezi.

THE LOWER ZAMBEZI

Descending from a higher-lying plateau and cutting numerous smaller gorges along the way, the river drops down and widens again before being joined by the Shire River, which drains from Lake Malawi, over 400 kilometres to the north. Choked by silt and flowing over flatter land, it becomes shallower and sluggish as it widens to eight kilometres in places, the widest it becomes throughout its course. Shortly before reaching the mouth, the river splits into two main channels to form a wide delta, fragmented by countless sandbars, swampy channels and mangrove stands. Having covered almost 650 kilometres from Cahora

Bassa, the Zambezi finally spills its waters through four outlets into the Indian Ocean.

RIVER CAPTURE

Over 100 000 years ago, which geologically is a fairly recent time frame, the Upper Zambezi was thought to have once been a separate river from the middle and lower sections. It had a southwesterly course that flowed into Lake Makgadikgadi, a superlake in excess of 60 000 square kilometres and possibly as large as 200 000 square kilometres; while the middle and lower sections had their headwaters somewhere below and north of Victoria Falls. Through one of two processes, possibly headwards erosion but more likely overtopping, and in association with tectonic movements in the earth's crust, the Upper Zambezi rose to a level that flowed into the basalt plateau, diverting the water onto the present course of the Middle Zambezi. Known as a **'river capture'**, this process joined two separate and average-sized river systems into one larger system. At a higher level, the waters of the upper river system forged the Victoria Falls and the gorges below before joining with the Middle Zambezi. This all took place in a period when rainfall levels were far higher, hence the size of the superlake, but because of the present drier period, the lake has since dried out.

The Victoria Falls

Often described as the **'largest curtain of falling water'** on the planet, Victoria Falls, particularly in full flood, is truly a sight to behold. Spanning the full breadth of the Zambezi River, the waterfall is listed as one of the Seven Natural Wonders of the World and as a World Heritage site, and is approximately twice as wide and double the depth of Niagara Falls. For many, it is Africa's most impressive and spectacular geographical feature.

Dr David Livingstone, the Scottish explorer and missionary, was the first European to announce the waterfall to the outside world. Led by two Makololo tribesmen paddling a traditional dugout canoe, he first laid eyes on the actual precipice on 16 November 1855, while standing on a small island, now known as Livingstone Island. Overawed by its majesty and might, he wrote, 'It [has] never been seen before by European eyes, but scenes so lovely must have been gazed upon by angels in their flight'. In honour of the Queen of England, Queen Victoria, he renamed it the Victoria Falls.

Before Livingstone and the subsequent influx of Europeans sightseers, the waterfall had, possibly for thousands of years, been celebrated by numerous groups of people. For these peoples, the site had a sacred and cultural significance and went by various different names. For the Tokaleya, the waterfall was known as 'Shongwe'; to the Ndebele, a group of Nguni who came later, it was 'Amanza Thunquayo'; and to the more recent Makololo people, they named the falls Mosi-oa-Tunya, 'the smoke that thunders' because of the high spray clouds and the thunderous noise of the falling water. The waterfall was also known to groups such as the Bayei, Lozi, Subiya and no doubt the San, the regions very earliest inhabitants.

Factfile – Victoria Falls

Due to the immense, erosive power of annual floodwaters pouring over the underlying rock, the formation of the Victoria Falls has come about over tens of thousands of years. The first processes began a lot earlier, somewhere near 100 million years ago, when cataclysmic crustal activity caused tears in the earth's surface. Boiling basaltic lava poured forth, and was deposited over time in thick layers, covering the region way beyond the present site. The cooling process was swift, causing points of weakness and long fissures, later filled with softer limestone sediments. By reading the preserved sedimentary layers lying both upstream and downstream of the waterfall, geologists believe, by comparison to the laying down of the rocks, the Zambezi's erosive powers began fairly recently, possibly a mere 100 000 years ago, but after the Upper Zambezi had been captured. As the river grew in size, flowing on a southerly course, the relentless water activity eroded along points of weakness lying on an east-west axis, firstly by removing the limestone deposits, and then cutting back into the harder basalt rock.

This process has repeated itself, with the largest volume of water flowing through the point of greatest vertical weakness. Depending on long-term water cycles, sediment load and hardness of the rock, the water eventually eroded the rock to a point where it started cutting back at the next weakest point and eroding a gorge below, thereby beginning the next fall line. Now onto its eighth successive fall line, the previous seven lie downstream in a wonderful zigzag pattern, showing clearly the previous abandoned waterfall positions in the Batoka Gorge. It is believed that the next cutback will be from the point now known as Devil's Cataract.

- The Victoria Falls lie almost 1 200 kilometres from the source of the Zambezi.
- The falls plunge over the Zambezi Gorge, a 1 708-metre-wide cliff edge, making it the greatest curtain of falling water on earth at peak flood times.
- On average, the water falls at over 500 million litres a minute at full flow, dropping to somewhere between 10 and 20 million litres a minute during the low season.
- Spray can rise almost 400 metres into the air and can be seen from 30 kilometres away.
- The present fall line is thought to be approximately 2 500 years old.
- Because of the narrowness of the gorge, a one-metre rise in water above the falls results in a five-metre rise in the gorge below.
- The main cataracts, starting from the western edge are known as Devil's Cataract, Main Falls (this is 830 metres wide), Horseshoe Cataract, Rainbow Falls, Armchair Cataract and Eastern Cataract (101 metres).
- The Rainbow Falls are the highest (108 metres) and Devil's Cataract the lowest at 63 metres. Two islands, Cataract and Livingstone, are situated in-between the cataracts.
- Together, the Victoria Falls National Park and the Mosi-oa-Tunya National Park on the Zambian side were proclaimed as a World Heritage site in 1989.
- The lowest water levels occur during October and November and the highest in March to May.
- The highest recorded flow was in 1958, when 700 million litres per minute was recorded.
- The Victoria Falls Bridge was completed in 1905 and stands roughly 130 metres above the water below. The steel construction is 250 metres across, with the main arch spanning 156.5 metres.

First proclaimed by local administrators as a 'Special Area' in 1935, the waterfall was upgraded to a reserve in 1937 before becoming a full National Park in 1952. In 1970 it was accorded National Monument status. While the waterfall is the main feature and attraction, it also consists of a rainforest dominated by ebony, mahogany, African olive and date palm trees. Heavily wooded, the park and the river are a haven for bird-watchers, with various turaco, hornbill and raptor species the highlights.

Kariba Dam

The Zambezi River has two massive dams along its course, Kariba in Zimbabwe and Cahora Bassa in Mozambique. Both were built as hydroelectric power schemes and with the build-up of water behind their walls, they have become hugely impressive lakes. Kariba was built in the Kariba Gorge, almost 600 kilometres downstream of Victoria Falls. The site was chosen ahead of an alternative one considered on the Kafue River in Zambia.

Kariba Factfile

- The tender was awarded to Impresit, an Italian consortium, and Kariba was designed by André Coyne, a French engineer who specialised in designing arch dams.
- The construction of the hydroelectric dam began in 1955. The first stage, Kariba South Power Station, was completed in 1959. It was officially opened in May 1960 by Queen Elizabeth, the Queen Mother. The Kariba North Power Station was completed only in 1977. At the time of building, the double curvature arch wall was the largest dam wall in the world.
- The dam is jointly owned by the Zimbabwean and Zambian governments and is managed by the Zambezi River Authority.
- The first stage cost approximately US$135 million and the second stage US$480 million.
- The dam wall is 128 metres high and 617 metres long. At its base it is 24 metres wide, which tapers to 13 metres at the top.
- Over 1 032 million cubic metres of concrete was used in the construction process.
- The dam wall holds a slipway consisting of six floodgates, each measuring 9 metres by 8,8 metres in size. At maximum flow, 136 billion litres of water per day pass through a single gate.
- Kariba is Africa's largest artificial lake, with the reservoir of water extending almost 290 kilometres upstream and covering an area of over 4 000 square kilometres. The volume of water has caused numerous earthquakes in the region, the most severe registering a magnitude of 6.1 on the Richter scale.
- The average depth of the lake is 20 metres and the deepest point reaches 120 metres.
- Eighty-six workers lost their lives in the construction of the dam.
- The backup of water created by the wall forced over 57 000 people, mostly from the Tonga group, to move to higher ground.
- Operation Noah, a rescue mission headed by Rupert Fothergill, was carried out in 1960 and 1961 to save wildlife from the rising waters. They resettled over 6 000 animals on higher ground, amongst these 44 rhinoceros, 23 elephant, 1 866 impala and 78 buffalo.
- Since its completion, the dam has spawned two major industries in the region. Tourism, particularly the renting of houseboats for fishing and game-viewing trips, was strong during the 1980s and 1990s. A second industry, that of kapenta fishing, provides a thriving business for dozens of fishing rigs that spend nights out on the lake, netting tons of a small, sardine-like species, the Lake Tanganyika sardine, *Limnothrissa miodon*. It is sold in markets throughout Southern and East Africa.

The Chobe River

While the Chobe can never be spoken of in the same terms as the Zambezi, it has its own **gentle appeal**. Sluggish and leisurely in comparison, time on its waters is more about soaking up the tranquillity and being able to observe the rich variety of wildlife that congregates along its banks.

Although the Chobe has a well-earned reputation as a premier safari destination, few realise that it is in fact only a small component of a larger, multifaceted system comprising numerous other features. Much like the Okavango Delta further to the south, this **greater integrated system**, often referred to as the Kwando/Linyati/Liambezi/Chobe System, owes its formation to ongoing tectonic activity and geological faulting associated with the Great Rift Valley. Millions of years ago, like the Zambezi, it was thought to have flowed in a southerly direction into Lake Makgadikgadi, but because of faulting in the earth's crust, the Linyanti and Chobe fault lines have redirected it onto its present easterly course and into the Zambezi River.

The source of the Chobe lies approximately 730 kilometres to the north, in the highlands of Angola, where its drainage basin covers almost 40 000 square kilometres. Flowing in an easterly and then southerly direction, it is known as the Rio Cuando as it passes through the fertile regions of south-eastern Angola. At the furthermost extremity of this country, it becomes the border with Zambia for nearly 230 kilometres before it enters the Caprivi Strip of Namibia, where the river

is known as the Kwando. Featureless and flat, the terrain slows the river's flow substantially as it enters the Linyanti Marsh, a 1 400 square kilometre mix of water channels, grassland floodplains and reed and papyrus beds together comprising Namibia's largest permanent wetland. Much of the inflowing flood waters are lost here, as shallow average depths and high vegetation cover result in high evapotranspiration levels. To the southeast of this system, less than 20 per cent of the floodwaters drain eastwards out of the Linyanti, as a river that becomes the border between Namibia and Botswana. Known as the Linyanti River, its flow is slow as it passes through a maze of swampy terrain to Lake Liambezi. From here, it becomes the Chobe as it meanders for approximately 60 kilometres across what is in effect an extended floodplain, before reaching its confluence with the Zambezi River, opposite the Botswana border town of Kasane.

It is a complex system that often defies conventional **flow directions**. Although flood waters arriving via the Kwando are at their highest from late May through to early August, the Chobe will at times receive water from the Zambezi in the reverse direction, when this river is experiencing particularly high flood levels. These waters push back up the Chobe, covering the floodplains and into Lake Liambezi. Another peculiarity is the Selinda Spillway, which in times of extreme flooding in the Okavango Delta, sees water being pushed into the Chobe from the channels of the northern Okavango.

Page 56: *Basaltic rock around Victoria Falls.* **Opposite:** *Fishermen on Lake Kariba.* **Below:** *The Chobe River from Chobe Chilwero Lodge.*

Victoria Falls town, or simply 'the Falls' to the locals, is routinely referred to in marketing jargon as the **'adrenaline capital'** of Africa. Although somewhat clichéd to some, there is no other description or phrase as apt as this to encapsulate the sense of what holidaying at Zimbabwe's most popular tourist spot is all about.

The grand spectacle will always be the hugely impressive Victoria Falls waterfall, the widest in the world and one of its Seven Natural Wonders – but once that has given you a right royal soaking, it is all about adrenaline sports and adventure options, most of which take place on or over the waters of the Zambezi River. Fed by surging waters that flow year round, the river provides endless opportunities for fun and excitement. While a few days are enough for some, it is also a destination that has a week's worth of choices.

Previous spread: *Victoria Falls has a 1 708-metre-wide cliff edge.*
Below: *The town of Victoria Falls.*

Totally tourism

Although the town has long been regarded as Zimbabwe's major tourism destination and boasts some of the country's **finest hotels and lodges**, its beginnings were rather less glamorous. Back in the late 1890s and a little upstream of the waterfall, the first small trading post along the river was established. Known as the Old Drift Trading Post, it comprised a collection of traders and unruly hawkers who had gathered at what was a new frontier in the expansion of British commercial and political interests in the region. This rough and rudimentary settlement was the precursor to Victoria Falls town.

At the time, Cecil John Rhodes and his British South Africa Company (BSAC) were the major colonial players in the region, and with them at the helm, the vision was to link Southern Rhodesia (now Zimbabwe) with Northern Rhodesia (now Zambia), where Rhodes was certain he would find great deposits of mineral wealth. There was, of course, also Rhodes's grand scheme of the Cape to Cairo railway line. Against the advice of locals, who preferred a spot further upstream, Rhodes himself chose the bridge site because he liked the idea of spray from the waterfall showering the crossing trains. He never did live to see his dream fulfilled, however – he died in 1902, two years before the line from Hwange reached the site of the present-day Victoria Falls in April 1904.

The wonder of the waterfall spread quickly, and it was only a few months later that the first steam trains began arriving with visitors, serving as the catalyst to the tourism industry and paving the way for the construction of the bridge. The **first hotel** followed shortly thereafter. Built to house construction workers, the Victoria Falls Hotel, a simple 16-roomed wooden and corrugated iron structure, opened months later in 1904. Present-day visitors will note the wild lion and sphinx logo of the hotel; a symbol of the hoped for Cape to Cairo railway line.

The famous **Victoria Falls Bridge**, spanning the gorge and linking Zimbabwe to Zambia, was connected and opened on 31 March 1905. The steel structure was designed by Sir Ralph Freeman, the engineer who also designed the Sydney Harbour Bridge, and his

company, Douglas Fox & Partners, and was built by the Cleveland Bridge & Engineering Company. The engineering masterpiece was constructed in England and the pieces shipped to Beira, Mozambique, before being transported to the present site. The cantilever design, with an arch span of 156.5 metres was then assembled simultaneously from opposite banks, using a cable and pulley system to move the materials from side to side; before being joined in the middle 14 months after construction began.

With the transport infrastructure in place and a growing list of people wanting to view the waterfall, some from as far afield as Cape Town, the tourism industry began to burgeon. In 1913, the Victoria Falls Hotel underwent an initial major upgrade, with the first brick structure being completed, and in 1935 the waterfall site was declared a national monument.

After a brief lapse during the Second World War, Victoria Falls received a massive endorsement in 1947 with the Royal visit of King George VI and Queen Elizabeth, when they booked out the entire hotel. Their stay put the town on the international tourism circuit, which was then further boosted by the introduction a short while later of a flying boat service between London and Victoria Falls.

The town's reputation continued to grow until the 1970s, when Zimbabwe became embroiled in its war of independence and the low intensity guerilla conflict became a deterrent to tourism. During this conflict, the bridge was used in 1975 as the venue for negotiations between the Rhodesian government and representatives of the liberation movements. Held aboard a carriage parked in the middle of the bridge, the attempted peace talks eventually failed, as then Prime Minister Ian Smith refused to grant immunity of prosecution to leaders returning from exile.

Independence came in 1980 and with it a return to peace, heralding a period of substantial growth through the 1980s and early 1990s. The Victoria Falls National Park, together with Mosi-oa-Tunya National Park on the Zambian side, were declared World Heritage sites in 1989 and numerous new large-scale hotels and lodges, including the Elephant Hills, Ilala Lodge, Victoria Falls

Safari Lodge and the Kingdom went up in and around the town. Attracting visitors from across the spectrum, the town basked in the glory of its heyday, labelled the 'adrenaline capital' of the world and a definite stopover on every safari itinerary to the region.

More recently, because of political and economic upheavals resulting from Zimbabwe's chaotic land reform programme, the town of Victoria Falls has endured a sharp decline in tourism.

WHERE TO STAY

As befits the status of a popular resort town, there is no shortage of accommodation options for visitors. Most are centrally located and those that are out of town offer convenient transport services throughout the day.

The Victoria Falls Hotel – After the waterfall itself, this large, colonial style hotel is the most famous landmark in town and for many, the place to stay – and with three great restaurants, tennis courts, a large swimming pool and the legendary afternoon tea patio overlooking sprawling gardens, why not? Built in the early 1900s, the style and décor reflect everything of the colonial era. Most of the rooms front onto the gardens and a view that overlooks the Batoka Gorge, the waterfalls spray cloud and the railway bridge. Tel: +263 13 4751/61, e-mail: reservations@tvfh.zimsun.co.zw

The Stanley and Livingstone – In many ways a mini version of the Victoria Falls Hotel, this extremely elegant and luxurious boutique hotel is the swankiest option in town. Situated on a private wildlife estate about 15 kilometres out, on the airport road, it also offers privacy and tranquillity. Tel: +263 13 41003/44557, e-mail: aujanzim@zol.co.zw

Ilala Lodge – This medium-sized hotel offers great value for money in comfortable and pleasant surroundings. Close to the centre of town and bordering on the Victoria Falls National Park, it is also ideally situated. Tel: +263 13 44737/44223, e-mail: ilalazws@africaonline.co.zw

Victoria Falls Safari Lodge – Although styled along the lines of a safari lodge, this is more a medium-sized hotel. Situated four kilometres from town on a private wildlife reserve that includes a floodlit waterhole for game viewing, it is a very popular choice with foreign visitors. Tel: +263 13 43211/2/3, e-mail: saflodge@saflodge.co.zw

The Victoria Falls Bridge as seen from the Victoria Falls Hotel.

Lokuthula Lodges – Situated in the same complex as the Victoria Falls Safari Lodge, this self-catering option has 37 units and offers the full array of amenities. Tel: +263 13 44717/44728, e-mail: loklodge@mweb.co.zw

The Kingdom – Next door to the Victoria Falls Hotel, this large and garish hotel complex is popular because of its casino and a choice of clubs and restaurants adjacent to the hotel. Tel: +263 13 42759, e-mail: reservations@kingdom.zim.co.zw

Elephant Hills – Although large and somewhat out of place, the Elephant Hills hotel complex does offer all the comforts and facilities. In addition, it has the only golf course in the region. Tel: +263 13 44793, e-mail: reservations@ehic.zimsun.co.zw

Amadeus Garden Guesthouse – Situated towards the back of the residential area, this clean and comfortable guesthouse is the best budget option in town. Tel: +263 13 42261, e-mail: info@insightafrica.de

Shoestrings – A large backpacker house and dormitory in the residential area, close to the centre of town. Tel: +263 13 40167, e-mail: sstrings@mweb.co.zw

Savanna Lodge – Another backpacker option, also in the residential area, but with a less rowdy atmosphere. Tel: +263 13 42821, e-mail: savann@telcovic.co.zw

THINGS TO DO

If you have come for rest and relaxation you have chosen well, but expect to be tempted by at least one of a multitude of exciting outdoor activities on offer. Contact the following two operators – between them they have all the options covered, and more. Both are situated on Parkway Drive in the centre of town.

Shearwater Adventures – +263 13 44471/ 43392/44483 or mobile +263 11 406668/ 406997, e-mail: reservations@shearwater.co.zw, website: www.shearwateradventures.com

Wild Horizons – +263 13 44571/44426 or mobile +263 11 208074, e-mail: info@wildhorizons.co.zw, website: www.wildhorizons.co.za

White water rafting – With grade five rapids for much of the way, spend a half- or full day rafting in some of the world's wildest and most famous white water. Be sure of your fitness though, as there is a fairly steep walk into the gorge and an even longer one out, and the chances are you will get to swim the rapids somewhere along the way.

Below, left: *Many consider the Zambezi River the world's best for white water rafting.* **Below, right:** *A kayaker riding the rapids in the Zambezi Gorge.*

Bungy jumping – No longer the world's highest, but in all likelihood, still the most popular. Follow the freefall of more than 110 000 other jumpers who have jumped before you – hurl yourself off the railway bridge and spend a few seconds plummeting the 111-metre drop.

High wire – Three mind-blowing, gut-wrenching adrenaline activities that will cement your faith in the art of cables and clips and those who keep them fastened – for the milder of heart, start on the 'flying fox' that takes you out horizontally for 200 metres across the gorge, suspended 120 metres above the river on a static cable. If speed is your thrill, jump onto the Foefie Slide and hurtle 425 metres across the gorge on a static cable, reaching speeds of just over 100 kilometres per hour. For the crazy bunch: simply leap over the edge and into a 70 metre freefall before the Gorge Swing kicks in and takes you out into a 95-metre swinging arc. For those of saner mind, there is the relatively sedate option of abseiling 120 metres down into the gorge. The lookout platform where all these activities take place is set on the very edge of the Batoka Gorge, between the railway bridge and the Victoria Falls Hotel.

Canoeing – A more tranquil option than rafting, a day's canoeing on the Upper Zambezi is no less thrilling. Hippo, crocodiles and a variety of bird species are ever-present, and there is always the possibility of encountering elephant, buffalo and a variety of antelope species. Operators also offer camp-out trips.

The bungy jump drops 111 metres off Victoria Falls Bridge.

Jet boating – For those who want a real close-up of the waterfall and an absolute drenching, this is your option. The power of these boats gets you up and over rapids three, two and one, and to within 30 metres or so of the main curtain of falling water. It's not for purists, though.

'Flight of Angels' – The falls are immensely impressive, so you may as well see them from every angle and height. Take to the air in either a micro light or helicopter for the most spectacular views of the waterfall, gorge and town.

Sundowner cruises – Once the exciting options are out of the way, pick a sundowner cruise that boats upstream of the falls and spend a few hours sipping cocktails and taking it all in. There are also breakfast and lunch cruise options available.

Golf – Every resort town has its golf course, but few offer the excitement of warthog, impala, bushbuck and the occasional elephant as additional hazards. In addition, the Elephant Hills course offers golfers a lush 18-hole layout.

Elephant Camp – Spend time with elephants, the most enchanting of beasts, either as a half-day option or overnight at the camp.

Falls Craft Village – Something of an institution in the town, this mock traditional village offers insights into the lifestyle of various ethnic groups by day, becoming a vibrant drumming and Makishi pole and stilt dancing venue by night. It is situated in the centre of town, near the Elephant Walk complex.

SHOPPING

Elephant Walk – Behind the main post office, this complex has a variety of stores selling artwork, pottery, clothing, beadwork and furniture. There is also a small coffee shop.

Trading Post – On Livingstone Way, this complex is the largest in town, with stores offering everything from crafts and clothing to music and artwork.

The Kingdom – Inside the casino complex there are a few up-market stores offering artwork, curios, clothing and related items. There is also a pharmacy, bank and Internet café.

The Craft Market – For those who love the art of the bargain, a large craft market behind the Elephant Walk offers everything from wood carvings, masks and soapstone pieces to fabrics, baskets and more.

Makishi dancers from the Falls Craft Village.

Above: *Zimbabweans are master soapstone sculptors.*

Opposite: *Drummers perform at The Boma restaurant in the Victoria Falls Safari Lodge.*

Page 71: *Traditional Zimbabwean dishes are offered at The Boma restaurant in the Victoria Falls Safari Lodge.*

Art for all

Botswana's name is synonymous with the subcontinent's most intricate and beautifully woven baskets, made mainly by the Bayei and Hambukushu women from the northwestern regions of the Okavango Delta. Zambia has a sampling of almost everything, but the best place within the region to look for artwork is in Victoria Falls town.

The Shona people are famed for their ironwork, pottery and **stone carving** abilities, while the Ndebele are the masters at woodwork. A rich variety of these items, plus leatherwork, wirework, beadwork and fabric of all types, are sold in every market and in almost every hotel and lodge. Despite all this choice, Zimbabwe is most strongly associated with its soapstone carvings. Often large and distorted, these masterpieces are carved from a variety of soft stones that go by names equally as colourful as the work itself: fruit serpentine, black serpentine, spring stone and verdite are some of the primary materials used. While originally carved by the Shona as expressions of their spiritual and **mystical world**, today many of the sculptors lean towards combining tradition with the social and political aspects of the modern world. Buyers of carvings should be aware that the material itself carries no intrinsic value, and that prices asked are merely a reflection of the artist's reputation and the amount of time put into the carving. For those wanting to export or ship carvings home, **be careful** not to buy the softest stones, like opal, as these have a tendency to crumble or break if not handled with extreme care.

Other traditional items include Tonga baskets (*munyumbwe* or *siampondo* baskets) with intricately woven patterns using fibre from the ilala palm; narrow cylindrical drums (*ngoma*); thumb pianos (*mbira*); wooden dishes and bowls (ndiro) that come in a variety of shapes and sizes; low-based Tonga stools with a circular concave seat (*zvigaro*) and wooden headrests or pillows (*mutsago*). Buyers of any of the above items should also consider asking the trader or guide about the wood type used, as it is a fact that some are carved from endangered tree species. While the artist should be entitled to make a living, it is preferable that this be done using a resource that is **sustainable**.

Good-quality paintings are harder to come by, and your best bet will be to look in these three places:

The Lucky Bin – Situated in the Trading Post complex on Livingstone Way, this small and easily overlooked gallery often has some fine paintings and etchings by Zimbabwean artists.

Prime Art Gallery – Located in the Elephant Walk Village, this gallery carries the work of artists from various African countries, while also focusing on Shona art.

The River Café – A small group of artists, including Sanele Dhlomo (see page 70), work from the space opposite the café. If you are in town for a while, they will readily take commissions to complete before you depart.

PROFILE – SANELE DHLOMO

Tall, handsome and dreadlocked, Sanele Dhlomo catches the eye amongst his fellow artists at the River Café in Victoria Falls. Once you have been lured to the jumble of easels, painting tables and trays, his work will captivate you. With immensely vivid colours and bold strokes, large oil and pastel portraits and canvases of contemporary township life are the standout pieces in the cooperative. For him, the work is simply an expression of Zimbabwean life, often with a humorous take or a slightly exaggerated focus. Sanele was born in Bulawayo, and his first brushstrokes were inspired by watching his older brother at work. He started with watercolours and sketches and after school, Tommy Ndebele, the well-known Zimbabwean artist, was his inspiration to venture into art school and paint large oils. In search of better sales and to broaden his horizons, Sanele moved to the Falls in 2000.

He has already had one exhibition in a Bulawayo gallery and has work displayed in various Victoria Falls hotels. For commissions, contact Sanele on saneledhlomo@hotmail.com or on his mobile: +263 11 506599, or just visit the River Café.

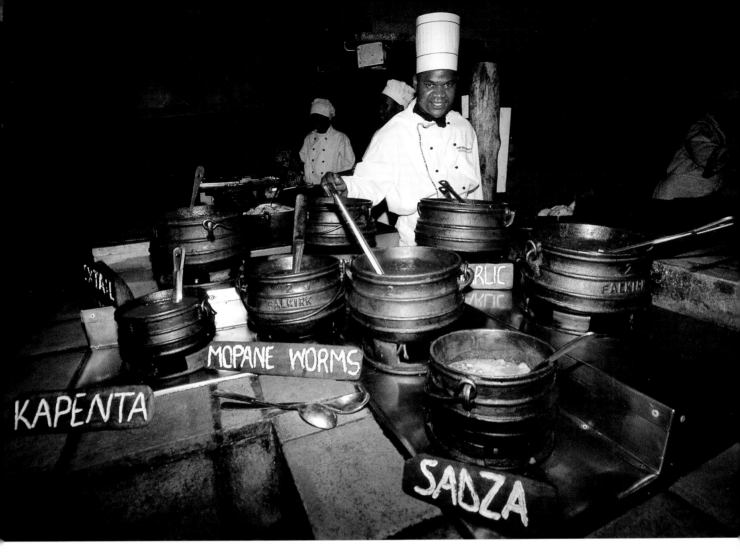

EATING OUT AND NIGHTLIFE

Mama Africa's Eating House – This funky, contemporary, township style restaurant behind the Trading Post complex is a must. On offer are a variety of African dishes and there is usually a resident band playing African jazz rhythms. Tel: +263 13 41725

The Boma – Adjacent to the Victoria Falls Safari Lodge, the Boma offers a great night out with a sumptuous variety of Zimbabwean dishes, traditional dancing and a rousing drumming finale to the evening. Booking is advised. Tel: +263 13 43238/43211

310 Parkway Tea Garden – Located at the end of Parkway, 310 offers breakfasts, lunches and dinners and some of the best coffee in town.

The River Café – A great meeting place in the Trading Post complex on Livingstone Way, the café offers breakfasts, light lunches and coffees, with satellite television.

Victoria Falls Hotel – Afternoon tea on the patio, overlooking the sprawling lawns, is an absolute must.

The Jungle Junction – This garden restaurant offers a fantastic outdoor buffet.

The Kingdom – This complex has a variety of restaurants ranging from pizza parlours and hamburger joints to **The Wild Thing**, a bar and nightclub offering light foods.

Croc Rock – If you want to shoot pool and party with the locals until dawn, head for this bar and nightclub behind the Soper Centre.

The Cattleman – Situated at the back of the Phumula Centre, this very reasonably priced restaurant and bar offers the best steaks in town.

LIVINGSTONE

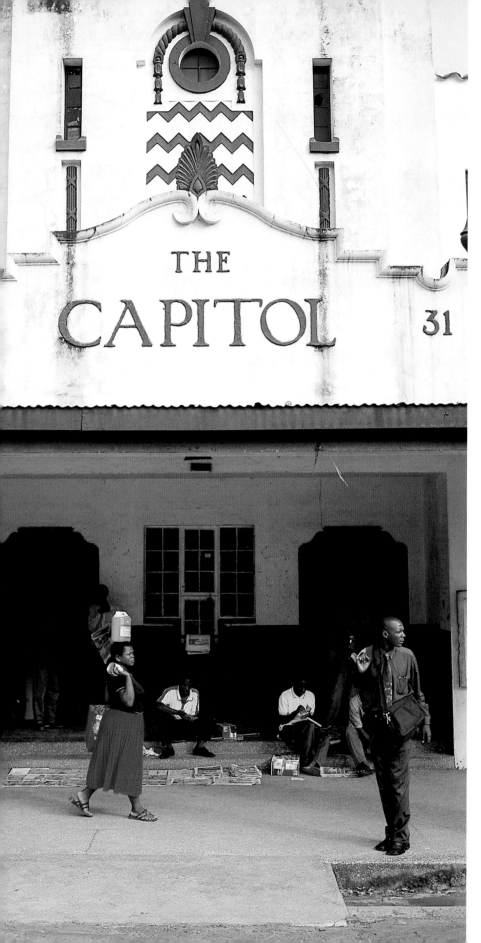

Zambia's tourism capital bears all the characteristics of a **bustling African town** boasting a strong colonial heritage. Its wide, tree-lined main road, now heavily potholed in places, is the hub. Along this entire route, a fascinating conglomeration of historic homes and buildings standing alongside rudimentary dwellings and shacks most vividly reflects the town's dual identity. Taking its name from David Livingstone, the famed explorer and missionary, its history goes back over 100 years and owes much to the activities of the then British colonial administration and the mining exploits of Cecil John Rhodes and his British South Africa Company (BSAC).

Although now one of Zambia's fastest growing centres, with developments sprouting everywhere, its growth path has been a somewhat chequered one. After an auspicious start through the decades of the early 1900s, when it was the territory's capital city, a near total collapse in fortunes followed after independence, before Livingstone began to re-emerge in the late 1990s and claim its title as the tourism capital of the country.

Today, with the tourism industry leading its economic growth, Livingstone is a **vibrant boom town** with a colourful and funky atmosphere. While the region has most certainly benefited from the woes of Zimbabwe, it is nonetheless an immensely tempting destination in its own right. Much of Livingstone's appeal lies in the diversity of attractions on offer, spanning its rich history. The cultural experiences and exciting adventure sports are all supported by a selection of great lodges and hotels.

From trading post to tourism capital

The Old Drift Trading Post, the same early settlement that gave life to the town of Victoria Falls, was also Livingstone's forerunner. Already established on the Zimbabwean side, it spread across the river in 1898, as the word went out that the hinterlands to the north held agricultural and mining riches. Prospectors, hunters and moneymen came in search of new opportunities, some to stake a claim while others simply catered to the ever-increasing number of convoys crossing the river from what became known as Southern Rhodesia. It was from these humble beginnings that Livingstone began to emerge. The catalyst for growth from malaria-infested trading post to a **regional capital** was a combination of economic and political factors. Cecil John Rhodes had already secured all the mineral rights in the greater region by offering the king of the Lozi people, Paramount Chief Lewanika, protection from the Matabele. Coal was soon discovered south of the Zambezi at Hwange and prompted by stories of vast mineral deposits in the far north, Rhodes and the BSAC built a railway line linking these two spheres of burgeoning wealth. By 1904, the line had reached Victoria Falls. Fourteen

Previous spread: *Mosi-oa-Tunya Street in Livingstone was designed to allow enough space for ox-wagons to make U-turns.*

Opposite: *Livingstone has some wonderful examples of old colonial architecture.* **Below:** *A street scene in the middle of Livingstone.*

MALINDI'S CAR WASH & GO BANANAS

WITH SMALL CAPABILITIES AND WITH OUR FAITH WE CAN DEFEAT THE GREATEST FINANCIAL GIANTS OF MODERN TIMES AND BECOME MULTI-MILLIONAIRES

Opposite: *Viewing the Victoria Falls from the Zambian side.* **Above:** *A mural in Livingstone offers hope to aspiring business people.*

months later the bridge was completed, linking (then) Southern Rhodesia to Northern Rhodesia. In 1905, the BSAC decided to move its offices away from the Old Drift site, giving life to present-day Livingstone.

This relocation was by no means a unanimous decision. The combination of the waterfall and the railway line had already been pinpointed as a major tourist attraction in the making. When it came to choosing the exact site for the new town, many of the townsfolk wanted to be a lot closer to the waterfall, in order to take advantage of what they considered to be a certain money-spinner. There were reputedly many disputes and much argument, but needless to say, they lost out to the power of Rhodes and his company, who preferred the present day site of higher ground away from the river. Soon after, the town was given official sanction when the British Government chose Livingstone to become the centre of its interests north of the Zambezi River.

By 1910 the town of Livingstone had grown to a population of over 300 and boasted a fine Government House, a court house, two hotels, a hospital and post office, a boat club, various churches and numerous shops and commercial businesses. True recognition came in 1911 when it became the capital of Northern Rhodesia, which it remained until 1935, before losing its status to Lusaka. Although the new capital and by now flourishing Copperbelt began eroding Livingstone's political influence, the town continued to grow as a small commercial centre and a major railway junction. At the height of its prominence in the 1950s and early 1960s, the town was a **thriving colonial outpost**, and because of the Victoria Falls, became known as the 'tourist capital'.

After independence in 1964, Livingstone began to die. A heavy dose of socialism, introduced by the first post-colonial government, saw the economic fortunes of the country in general, and the tourism revenues of Livingstone in particular, begin to wane. The town was dealt a further blow by Zimbabwe's independence in 1980, which brought international recognition to its neighbour and put Victoria Falls town on the global tourist map. While Victoria Falls thrived throughout the 1980s and well into the 1990s, Livingstone was nothing more than a decaying ghost town. In 1991, Zambia held its first multiparty elections and with the fundamental changes to the political system came a fresh economic direction, which again began to breathe life into Livingstone. The awakening was gentle at first, but in a dramatic reversal of history, the real boom kicked in from 2000 when Zimbabwe commenced its calamitous political and economic slide.

WHERE TO STAY

Unlike Victoria Falls, where most accommodation options are situated in or very close to town, Livingstone has its best selection strung out along the Zambezi River. No matter how far away from the centre, convenient transport services are provided by all lodges during the day.

Sindabezi – This absolute gem of a hideaway is tucked away on a small private island in the midst of the Zambezi River. Simple and rustic, yet extremely comfortable, Sindabezi oozes charm, romance and tranquillity. Tel: +260 97 771488, e-mail: reservations@tongabezi.com

The River Club – This luxurious lodge is situated on a broad, sweeping bend of the Zambezi, downstream of the Falls. Standout features include the main building, distinctly Edwardian in style, the striking views from the chalets and swimming pool, and croquet on the grass lawns. Tel: + 260 3 324457

Taita Falcon Lodge – With the most stunning sites about 15 kilometres out of town, along the edge of the Batoka Gorge above rapids 16 and 17, this is the choice mid-market lodge outside the centre. The spacious and comfortable chalets complement the most

The view from the bathroom at Songwe Village.

wonderful views, and owner managed, the atmosphere is pleasantly homely. Tel: +263 11 208387, e-mail: taita-falcon@zamnet.zm

Songwe Village – Also perched atop the Batoka Gorge, with inspiring views, Songwe offers a traditional village experience that gives guests an insight into the life of the rural Tonga people. Tel: +260 977 853053, e-mail: reservations@kwando.co.za

Tongabezi – Arguably the regions most well-known lodge, Tongabezi was the first luxury option along the Zambezi and set the standards for everyone else to follow. It is still an excellent option at the very top-end of the market. Tel: +260 97 771488, e-mail: reservations@tongabezi.com

Islands of Siankaba – About 40 kilometres upstream, this elegant and well-sited lodge comprises two heavily wooded islands linked by a number of hanging bridges.

It is a great option for those wanting to be away from the hustle but closer to Livingstone. Tel: +260 3 324490 or 9 7791241, e-mail: siankaba@zamnet.zm

The Royal Livingstone – This is Zambia's premier large hotel. Elegant, and with a touch of the colonial in its styling, it has the finest of garden settings within sight of the waterfall and offers all the comforts and conveniences of a 5-star operation. Tel: +260 3 321122, e-mail: suninzam@zamnet.com

Zambezi Sun – Larger and with a more contemporary African style, this 3-star hotel has full conference facilities, and is adjacent to the Royal Livingstone within the same grounds. Tel: +260 3 321122, e-mail: suninzam@zamnet.com

Fawlty Towers – This guesthouse along Mosi-oa-Tunya Road has become one of Livingstone's most well-known landmarks, and is the best middle-market

A room with a view – Sindabezi Island.

option in town. It comes with a great swimming pool, a substantial, shaded garden and is adjacent to Hippo's restaurant. There is also a backpacker's house on an adjacent property. Tel: +260 3 323432, e-mail: ahorizon@zamnet.zm

The Waterfront – As the name suggests, this complex is situated within lush gardens on the banks of the Zambezi, between the town and the waterfall. It offers a range of accommodation from mid-priced chalets to tents and camping, also a restaurant and a great sundowner pub and deck. Tel: +260 3 320606/7, e-mail: zaminfo@safpar.com

Maramba River Lodge – Situated along the banks of the Maramba River, a short distance from the Falls, this mid-priced option offers chalets, tents and camping in spacious and pleasant grounds. Tel: +260 3 324189, e-mail: maramba@zamnet.zm

Jungle Junction – About 55 kilometres upstream of Livingstone, any backpackers and eternal travellers worth their walking boots will have this island hangout on the agenda. Something of an institution, it is rustic by design and very mellow in nature, so much so that fellow islanders have been known to stay and stay and stay ... Tel: +260 3 323798, e-mail: jungle@zamnet.zm

Jollyboys – This clean and comfortable backpacker's lodge is situated behind the Livingstone Museum. Tel: +260 3 324229, e-mail: jollyboys@zamnet.zm

THINGS TO DO

Unbeknown to most visitors, nearly all the adrenaline activities, bar parachuting, were pioneered on the Zambian side. This includes the first bungy jumping, abseiling and commercial rafting operations, to kayaking, river boarding and micro lighting. The association, though, has tended to be with Victoria Falls town because of the boom in tourism that Zimbabwe enjoyed during the 1990s. Livingstone still offers almost the same menu of exciting outdoor activities – but if these activities bore you, then take to the streets of town and soak up the mix of old and new as you mingle with some of the friendliest people anyone could hope to meet.

Contact the following three operators; between them they have all the options covered, and more.

Batoka Sky – Find them off the road that leads down to the Waterfront. Tel: +260 3 320058 or 11 409578, e-mail: freedom@zamnet.zm, website: www.batokasky.com

Bundu Adventures – They are situated on Industrial Road, off Mosi-oa-Tunya Road. Tel: +260 3 324407/8, e-mail: zambezi@zamnet.zm, website: www.bundu-adventures.com

African Horizons – They operate from Fawlty Towers on Mosi-oa-Tunya Road (see page 79). Tel: +260 3 323432, e-mail: ahorizon@zamnet.zm, website: www.adventure-africa.com

White water rafting – Operators on the Zambian side raft the same waters as their Zimbabwean counterparts, so it is as exciting and adventurous. Choose a half-day or full day and be sure of your fitness, as there is a fairly steep walk into the gorge and an even longer one out, and the chances are you will get to swim the rapids somewhere along the way.

Bungy jumping – No longer the world's highest, but in all likelihood still the most popular, follow the freefall of more than 110 000 other jumpers who have leapt before you and hurl yourself off the railway bridge to spend a few glorious angst-seconds plummeting the 111-metre drop.

The Zambezi Swing –The first high wire and abseiling venue in the region, it offers a variety of exhilarating adrenaline options from their site on the very edge of the gorge, about 15 kilometres out of Livingstone. The biggest rush is the Gorge Swing, a 53-metre free fall before you are taken out in a swinging arc above the treetops of the lower gorge. For sheer exhilaration, try the Cable Slide, which will whizz you down and across the gorge for 330 metres at speeds nearing 100 kilometres per hour. The High Wire, a more sedate option, is a foefie slide and flying fox combo that stretches 135 metres across the gorge over 90 metres above. The abseiling option covers more than 50 metres of sheer cliff face.

Canoeing – A more tranquil option than rafting, a day's canoeing on the Upper Zambezi is no less thrilling. Hippo, crocodile and a variety of bird species are ever present, and there is always the possibility of encountering elephant, buffalo and a variety of antelope species. Operators also offer camp out trips.

Jet boating – For those who want a real close-up of the waterfall, and an absolute drenching, this is your

Left, top: *Rafting with Bundu Adventures from the Zambian side.*
Left: *An evening river cruise on the African Princess.*

Above and opposite, left: *Shopping at the Falls Craft Market outside Livingstone.*

option. Available only when the river is fuller, the power of these boats gets you up and over rapids 3, 2 and 1, and to within 30 metres or so of the main curtain of falling water.

'Flight of Angels' – The falls are massively impressive, so you may as well see them from every angle and height. Take to the air in either a micro light or helicopter for the most spectacular views of the waterfall, gorge and town.

Sundowner cruises – If you have a choice, taking your sundowner cruise from Zambia is a better bet. Their side of the river is more scenic and they have closer access to the waterfall and its spray plume. There are numerous options, but the *African Queen* is the mother of all cruises. Operators also offer breakfast, lunch and full day cruises.

'Take a walk on the wild side' –This is the best way to see Mosi-oa-Tunya National Park and its small white rhino population. You are also likely to see various plains game species, and the birding is rewarding.

Horse riding – Follow the gorge edge out and back, for another option for the park.

Livingstone Museum – Amongst exhibits on local arts, crafts and natural history, the museum offers visitors a fascinating and informative insight into the colonial heritage of the greater region and also contains a collection of memorabilia belonging to David Livingstone, including personal letters and diaries.

Maramba Market – At the back of town, this major market has all the hustle, bustle and colour of a typical African market. It offers everything from food, clothing and traditional medicines to haircuts and on-the-spot mechanics.

Makuni Village – The nearby Makuni Village and its inhabitants offer visitors a warm and welcoming stroll through a maze of huts, and the chance to get involved in their daily lives. With a little luck you may also bump into Chief Makuni himself.

SHOPPING

Kubu Crafts – Situated on Mosi-oa-Tunya Road, this is the largest and most well known of the local craft outlets. As a retail outlet, they carry an extensive range of arts and crafts that includes locally made furniture and fittings. As manufacturers, they will custom make almost anything on order. They also have a garden coffee shop.

African Visions – Another great venue with a garden coffee shop. Also situated on Mosi-oa-Tunya Road, the shop offers a wide selection of African art, crafts and curios, and serves as a bookstore.

Makuni Park Market – Situated in Livingstone's central park, this is the largest African craft market in town, offering the usual selection of carvings, hangings, baskets and curios. Bargain hard, and be careful of pickpockets.

The Falls Activity Centre – Adjacent to the Zambezi Sun Hotel, this complex offers a selection of small craft stores, coffee shops, the hotel's activity centre and a restaurant. Be warned though; prices here are somewhat over the top.

The Falls Craft Market – Situated at the Zambian entrance to the Victoria Falls, immediately after the border post, it offers a similar selection to the Makuni Park Market, but at higher prices.

PROFILE – ALI SHENTON

Communities in the throes of regeneration so often have a few standout individuals who are central to the energy and drive that sustains their growth. Ali Shenton has been in town since Livingstone began its renewal and remains one of its most well-known and colourful characters.

Born in Lusaka and brought up in the Kafue, her father was warden of the national park. Although Ali has a degree in African Politics and Development Studies, and a diploma in journalism, she chose a life in the bush. The Luangwa Valley became home, where Ali ran her own craft workshop and involved herself in running safaris with her brother Derek. But after a decade and more, she hankered for a change in lifestyle, and sensing a shift in Livingstone's fortunes, Ali headed south in 1997. Within 24 hours of arriving, she had signed a lease on a shop and opened African Visions, one of Livingstone's first curio, craft and art outlets. The business has since grown, and now occupies a landmark house on Mosi-oa-Tunya Road that includes the region's only vegetarian restaurant and a second-hand bookstore.

Outside of running her businesses, much of her spare time is taken up by her work as Vice-Chairperson of the Livingstone branch of the Wildlife Environmental Conservation Society of Zambia. Ali is also a keen and highly talented artist (she spent two years at a Swedish art school), and this is a pastime she would dearly love to pursue in the future.

Above, left: *Lunch time at Sindabezi Island.* **Above, right:** *A vegetable vendor in the Maramba Market in Livingstone.*

EATING OUT AND NIGHTLIFE

African Visions – Conveniently located on Mosi-oa-Tunya Road, this fantastic vegetarian restaurant and coffee shop is situated in the same house as a craft shop.

Hippo's – Behind Fawlty Towers, this bar, restaurant and sometimes club offers a value-for-money menu of standard dishes.

Zigzag Coffee House – This coffee shop and restaurant offers good breakfasts and light lunches.

Ocean Basket – Situated on Mosi-oa-Tunya Road, the only seafood option in town has a large and spacious layout and carries a great menu.

Fez Bar – Enjoy typical pub fare and atmosphere amongst the local ex-pats.

Kamuza Restaurant – Situated in Ngolide Lodge, this small restaurant offers the best curries in town.

Rite Pub & Grill – Head this way if you want to drink and party with the locals. There is usually a great vibe and they often have local or visiting bands playing. It is situated right in the centre of town.

Beyond Livingstone

If the Caprivi Strip in Namibia or Mongu, the capital of Barotseland in western Zambia, is next on your route, head out of Livingstone on the Sesheke road. Once amongst the worst in Zambia, this 190-kilometre road has recently been fully upgraded, and the old ferry across the Zambezi to Katimo Malilo has now been replaced with an impressive 800-metre long bridge. Mongu and the Zambezi floodplains are another 320 kilometres further north (see 'Out of the Way' page 128), but for the faint of heart, bear in mind that this road has not been upgraded and still remains a testing journey on both vehicle and mind.

SHACKLETONS

The last haven before leaving western Zambia is **Shackletons**, a rustic and charming lodge overlooking a tranquil oxbow extension of the Zambezi River. The turn is approximately 140 kilometres from Livingstone, before three kilometres of dirt road lead into the lush gardens surrounding the chalets and campsite of Shackletons. Broken in places by smaller meandering channels and oxbow lagoons, the wide waters of this section of the Zambezi offer some of the best bream and tiger fishing to be found along the upper stretch of the river. While fishing is good all year round, May to December are the most rewarding months and both lure and fly-fishermen are catered for, as long as the catch-and-release policy is adhered to. The region is also a great birding destination, particularly during the summer months. For those who are water weary, there is the nearby **Mwandi Mission**. Built in the 1870s by French missionaries, the station hosts a variety of churches, a hospital and a number of schools and provides an interesting insight to the early colonial history of the region.

SEKOMA ISLAND

This mid-market island camp offers another great fishing and birding option along the Sesheke road. Well-hidden in dense, riverine forest on a private island near the confluence of the Zambezi and Chobe rivers, **Sekoma Island** is a great base from which to explore the surrounding waterways. Trips to Chobe National Park and Victoria Falls can also be arranged. While the island is best accessed by boat from the Kasane (Botswana) side, it can be reached by road on the Zambian side. Take the Mambova road that turns off the Kazangulu ferry road and follow the dirt track for about 10 kilometres to the village of Mambova. Either way, you will need to contact Desert & Delta Safaris to make arrangements.

Sekoma Island, near the confluence of the Chobe and Zambezi rivers.

KASANE

Kasane, Botswana's busiest tourism centre, lies in the far northeastern corner of the country, and while the town itself is not particularly impressive, it is the gateway to the Chobe National Park, one of the region's most popular wildlife destinations. The town also lies at a **crossroads** for those heading to Victoria Falls from the south and west of the sub-continent; and to Namibia from the east. Because of Zimbabwe's woes, the route running from Francistown to Kasane via Nata has become a very popular one for those heading north into central Africa.

Spread out along the banks of the Chobe River, Kasane has a number of hotels, guesthouses and campsites that continuously feed visitors into the national park. Most of the accommodation fronts onto the Chobe River and offers pleasant and tranquil surroundings. For those merely passing through, time here is usually a one-night stopover for fuel and other supplies.

Anyone heading for Livingstone in Zambia by road from Kasane will have to cross the river using the Kazangula Ferry, situated approximately 12 kilometres east of town. Don't be put off by the queues of trucks, just drive straight to the front.

WHERE TO STAY

If you have the budget, try **Chobe Chilwero** or **Chobe Game Lodge**, both of which are situated inside the park (see page 105). Otherwise any one of the following makes for a pleasant base:

Kubu Lodge – Offering smaller, lodge-type accommodation at the quieter end of the river, the lodge is closest to the Kazangula Ferry and also has camping facilities. Tel: +267 6250312, e-mail: kubu@botsnet.bw

Chobe Marina Lodge – Centrally situated, Kasane's newest large hotel has tranquil settings, a choice of two good restaurants and conference facilities. Tel: +267 6252221, e-mail: reservations@chobe.botsnet.bw

Chobe Safari Lodge – One of the old favourites on the banks of the river, it is the closest option to the park. There is a large hotel or chalets and a campsite with a neat sunset deck, overlooking the water. Tel: +267 6250336, e-mail: reservations@chobelodge.co.bw

The Garden Lodge – Situated centrally along the river, this smaller guesthouse option has a more intimate feel than the larger hotels. Tel: +267 6250051, e-mail: gabi@botsnet.bw

THINGS TO DO

Kasane is really only about safari options. Your best bet for advice on anything and everything to do and see in the greater Kasane, Chobe and Caprivi regions, is the **Chobe Travel Shop** – Tel: +267 6251754, e-mail: travel@botsnet.bw, website: www.chobetravel.com

Previous spread: *This well-known billboard greets visitors to Kasane as they leave the local airport.*
Opposite and left: *Fishing is the major economic activity for many families in the Kasane district. .*

on SAFARI

It is a simple truth of the safari world that no matter where in Southern Africa an itinerary is focused, Victoria Falls is almost always either the starting or finishing point. If the Falls is already on your radar, why not **alter conventional thinking**? Consider making the greater region your destination by including a selection of the many superb national parks and wildlife areas that surround the Falls. With the area served by three international airports, Livingstone, Victoria Falls and Kasane, all are within convenient reach.

In Zimbabwe, Hwange and Matetsi have well-established reputations, and despite the country's political and economic tribulations, they continue to enjoy a steady stream of visitors. Only slightly further afield, Chizarira and Matusadona offer more secluded and adventurous options. Mana Pools, while for some an 'out of the way'

choice, is most certainly worthy of consideration for its immense beauty and the quality of its wildlife sightings.

For those looking at day excursions and walking tours only, Zambezi National Park and Mosi-oa-Tunya National Park lie on the very doorstep of Victoria Falls and Livingstone respectively.

In Zambia, Kafue is one of Africa's largest and most diverse parks and with the recent opening of a northern circuit, it is now a full destination in itself.

In any preliminary research, Chobe in Botswana will surely have cropped up as a definite, and rightly so.

There is certainly no shortage of choice, and together, these wilderness options offer great beauty, a stunning diversity of animal and plant life, and are unlikely to have the volumes of visitors found elsewhere in Southern Africa.

National parks and reserves

In Zimbabwe, national parks account for 7.9 per cent of the land with a further seven per cent falling under forest reserves and the protection of private management. The national body is the Zimbabwe Parks and Wildlife Management Authority (www.zimparks.com). Zambia has nineteen national parks and game reserves, and together with numerous Game Management Areas (GMAs), 30 per cent plus of the country's land is protected in some way. These areas are managed by the Zambia Wildlife Authority (www.zambiatourism.com).

In Botswana, just over 17 per cent of land has been set aside for national parks and game reserves, managed by the Department of Wildlife and National Parks (DWNP). Added to the numerous forest reserves and private concessions, an impressive 39 per cent of land is protected in some form, including almost the entire northern third of the country (www.botswana-tourism.gov).

The main national parks that fall within the region are as follows:

Chobe National Park (Botswana)	11 700 sq km
Kafue National Park (Zambia)	22 480 sq km
Mosi-oa-Tunya National Park (Zambia)	66 sq km
Hwange National Park (Zimbabwe)	14 651 sq km
Chizarira National Park (Zimbabwe)	2 000 sq km
Matusudona National Park (Zimbabwe)	1 407 sq km
Mana Pools National Park (Zimbabwe)	2 190 sq km
Victoria Falls and Zambezi National Parks (Zimbabwe)	56 000 ha

Previous spread: *Game viewing in the Makololo concession, Hwange National Park.*
Opposite: *A summer storm sweeps across Hwange National Park.*
Below: *Elephant crossing the main road are a common sight for motorists travelling to and from Kasane in Botswana.*

TRANSFRONTIER CONSERVATION

The ideal of creating Transfrontier Conservation Areas (TFCAs) in Southern Africa is a more recent conservation initiative that has primarily come about as wildlife managers seek a solution to the region's growing elephant populations. Sometimes also referred to as Peace Parks or megaparks, the concept seeks to link national parks and wilderness areas, located within close proximity of each other, regardless of international boundaries, into substantially larger cross-border areas for elephants and other species to roam. One of the continent's most promising TFCAs is the proposed **Kavango-Zambezi megapark**, planned to link Chobe, Hwange and Kafue with the Okavango Delta in Botswana and various protected areas in southeastern Angola and Namibia's Caprivi Strip. If implemented, this would cover over 300 000 square kilometres and include more than 20 protected areas in five countries.

Below: *A chacma baboon sits as a sentinel atop a fan palm.* **Opposite:** *Linkwasha Camp in Hwange National Park.*

Wildlife highlights

- The region carries Africa's **densest elephant** population, with most estimates putting the number of animals somewhere between 80 000 and 120 000 during the dry season. Chobe National Park (particularly along the riverfront), Hwange, Matetsi and Mana Pools offer the most rewarding viewing, and while the dry months from May to October are best, elephant is seen throughout the year. Elephant can also be viewed in Chizarira, Mosi-oa-Tunya and Zambezi National Park.

- For the **big cats**, Chobe in Botswana and Hwange in Zimbabwe are the best destinations. While lions are regularly seen in both parks, leopard and cheetah sightings are less common. Kafue has more regular sightings of cheetah and is renowned for its leopards, particularly in the northern sector.

- Mosi-oa-Tunya National Park, bordering Livingstone, is the only place within the region to see **white rhino**. Operators from Livingstone offer the most exciting option: a half-day walk in the park. Poaching has decimated the populations that used to be found in the region's large parks.

- Chobe, Hwange, Matetsi, Mana Pools and Matusadona all have healthy **buffalo** populations, while the Kafue population is fast recovering.

- Roan and sable **antelope** are two of the most sought-after plains game species and both occur in the region, with Matetsi and Hwange offering the best sightings. Puku are another special species of the area, with the best chances of sightings in Kafue and Chobe.

- With its diversity of habitats, the region offers birders an amazing variety of species. While **birding** is excellent throughout the year, the summer months are the most rewarding, as all the migrant species are present. Specialties along the river systems include African skimmer, African finfoot, Pels fishing owl, whitebacked night heron and rock pratincole. In the gorge below Victoria Falls, taita falcon may be seen in the latter months of the year, and northern Kafue is well known for its wattled and crowned crane populations.

- Both the Chobe and Zambezi rivers have healthy populations of **crocodile** and **hippo**, and the Busanga Plains in Kafue have a growing number of hippo.

- Although **wild dogs** are rare within the region's national parks, sightings are possible in Hwange, Matetsi and Chobe.

In Zimbabwe

Despite recent troubled times, if you are travelling with a recognised operator, Zimbabwe remains a relatively safe and trouble free destination to visit. In fact, some would say that because of falling tourist numbers, places like Hwange, Matetsi and Mana Pools are now at their best, as most of the lodges and camps are not at full occupancy. The national parks also operate self-contained options consisting of chalets and campsites. To enquire about further details and make bookings, contact the Zimbabwe Parks and Wildlife Management Authority in Harare. Tel: +263 4 706077/8 or 707624/9, e-mail: natparks@africaonline.co.zw

HWANGE NATIONAL PARK

Hwange is in almost every sense Zimbabwe's most **prestigious national park**. Situated in the northwestern corner of Matabeleland, abutting Botswana's eastern border, the 14 651 square kilometre park is enveloped by the Matetsi concessions and hunting blocs to the north, and various private concessions and the Gwayi Conservancy to the east. This makes the region the country's largest tract of wilderness. To the west, Botswana's Chobe National Park and various forest reserves run the length of its border. With a species list of over 1 000 plants, 110 mammals and 410 birds, Hwange also carries the greatest diversity of life, and outside of the Victoria Falls National Park, receives the most visitors of all parks and reserves in Zimbabwe.

While the San people would have been the region's earliest inhabitants, during the centuries prior to the arrival of the first European settlers, the region was home to the Nambia people, a small group of Shona speakers (the park takes its name from one of their chiefs). During the larger part of the nineteenth century, they also shared their resources with the Ndebele people, who used the area as a royal hunting ground for their kings. The Ndebele were defeated by colonial forces in the late 1800s, heralding an era of overexploitation, as hunters, loggers and ivory traders moved in to claim Hwange's riches. Sensing the complete depletion of the

During extreme hot spells, guests to Linkwasha Camp need not venture beyond the swimming pool.

Walking amongst false
mopane trees in Hwange
National Park.

region's wildlife populations, the authorities proclaimed the Wankie Game Reserve (this corrupted version of Hwange was the park's name under colonial rule) in 1928, with Ted Davidson as its first warden. It was only decades later that the game began recovering, no doubt gaining impetus from the first artificial water points the authorities had begun installing. In 1949, Hwange's status was upgraded to that of a full national park.

Geographically, the park falls on the eastern edge of the Kalahari sand mantle, the largest unbroken mass of sand existing on the planet. Locally, the park comprises **two distinct regions**: the ancient basalt outcrops that occur in the north and act as the watershed for many of the drainage systems; and the remaining two-thirds of flat land that is covered by the Kalahari sands. Over millions of years these sands have been relentlessly eroded from higher lying areas and deposited over the underlying Karoo bedrocks found at depths of up to 300 metres below. Various tributaries feeding into the Deka, Lukosi and Gwayi river systems – the most reliable water supplies within the park – cut the northern sector.

These sandy soils are covered mainly by mixed woodland and savannah grassland, with Zambezi teak (*baikiaea plirijuga*), rosewood (*guibortia coleosperma*), ordeal trees (*erythrophleum africanum*) and bloodwood or kiaat (*pterocarpus angolensis*) dominating. Characteristic open clearings of short grasses and stands of tall ilala palms break the woodland areas. Mopane woodland (*colophospermum mopane*), interspersed with baobabs and ribbons of riverine forest spanning the riverbanks, dominate the northern third of the park.

Hwange is elephant country, with upwards of 20 000 the feature attraction for visitors. The park also has healthy populations of buffalo, giraffe, zebra and eland, and is well known for its sightings of rare sable and roan antelope. The cat predators are regularly seen and there are a number of wild dog packs resident in the park. The best game viewing is most certainly in the private concessions of **Linkwasha** and **Makololo**, both situated in the southern regions of the park. Each concession has a choice of two first-rate tented camps, offering all the rustic luxuries in the best of safari traditions. All four camps offer game drives and walks.

While the dry winter months are always regarded as the prime game-viewing period, the period from November through to late January is most certainly worth considering for its impressive scenery and summer skies. Awesome thundercloud formations provide the backdrop, and goaded by the annual rains, dusty brown landscapes give way to a palette of greens as the season progresses. For **self-drive visitors**, it is advisable to travel in a 4x4 vehicle. The main entrance gate is an easy two hour drive south of Victoria Falls and there are three major public camp sites: Robins Camp, Main Camp and Sinamatella, all in the far north of the park. They offer camping and self-catering chalets, and can be booked through the Zimbabwe Parks and Wildlife Management Authority (reservations: natparks@africaonline.co.zw).

Left: *Summer storm clouds gather over Hwange National Park.*
Right: *On safari in the Matetsi Private Game Reserve in Zimbabwe.*

Zimbabwe camps. Courteney's grandfather was part of the construction team that built the perimeter veterinary fence in the early 1950s. His father assisted national parks in the 1960s with game capture and his older brother worked as a professional guide from Makololo during the 1990s.

Courteney's position in the company and his love for Zimbabwe has taken him to every corner of the country but Hwange remains his first passion. Besides guiding and his senior managerial role within Wilderness Safaris, he spends much of his time working closely with the parks management authority on anti-poaching measures, borehole and road maintenance and community projects. This includes substantial financial and logistical support from Wilderness Safaris and their guests to a community bordering the Linkwasha Concession. Courteney is also one of a handful of non-veterinarians in the country who has a dangerous drugs licence, a step he took to help the parks rangers with the desnaring of wildlife.

Despite Zimbabwe's present troubled times, for him there is no doubt that in the not-too-distant future, the country will re-enter the fold of leading safari destinations. In the meantime, he remains committed to making a contribution towards keeping Hwange intact. Courteney is also an accomplished amateur wildlife photographer (some of his images appear in this book). He has his private pilot's licence and is a keen fly-fisherman.

COURTENEY JOHNSON

Continuing a long and distinguished association his family has had with the country's largest national park, Courteney Johnson has spent his entire professional guiding career in Hwange National Park, the last three as General Manager of Wilderness Safaris

MATETSI

Fronting onto the Zambezi River and extending the 70 kilometres between Victoria Falls and the Botswana border are the Matetsi concessions, a mix of private photographic and hunting blocs. Forming part of a greater conservation area with wildlife populations that are largely free roaming, Matetsi is flanked by Chobe National Park to the west, the Zambezi National Park to the east and Hwange National Park to the south.

The prime location is the **Matetsi Private Game Reserve**, a 50 000-hectare tract of floodplain and woodland wilderness leading onto the Zambezi River. Established in 1995, the reserve is run by CC Africa and is now a flourishing photographic area in what was once

a hunting bloc. The concession has two well-located luxury lodges, **Matetsi Water Lodge**, with prime riverfront views, and **Matetsi Safari Camp**, set amongst teak woodland and overlooking a pan approximately 18 kilometres inland. While Matetsi offers excellent elephant viewing, particularly during the dry winter months and into early summer, and also has good populations of the general plains game species, it is best known for sightings of sable antelope. Nowhere in Southern Africa are they common. Regarded by many as the most impressive of the antelope species, their jet black coats, striking horns and facial markings make them particularly conspicuous in the dry winter months, as the herds move from the woodland areas to the riverfront to drink.

Above: *The rolling hills of Chizarira National Park.* **Opposite:** *Canoeing in the Victoria Falls National Park.*

For those seeking a budget option along this section of riverfront, or an overnight stop between Kasane and Victoria Falls, **Imbabala Safari Camp** is a great choice. Situated a mere three kilometres from the Botswana border post and with panoramic views over the Zambezi River, the camp offers game drives into the surrounding concessions and river cruises along the Zambezi.

CHIZARIRA NATIONAL PARK
Wild, remote and accessible only with a 4x4 vehicle, Chizarira is a destination perfectly suited for self-drive enthusiasts and those wanting to move beyond the more well-trodden parks and reserves. Although lying between Kariba and Victoria Falls, two of Zimbabwe's busiest tourist hubs, Chizarira has remained somewhat isolated and relatively undeveloped, much to the delight of those who view the region as one of Zimbabwe's most pleasant. Getting there requires a sturdy vehicle and

a thorough knowledge of the local dirt road network, but once among the cliff faces and brachystegia and mopane woodland of the Zambezi escarpment, the journey becomes thoroughly worthwhile.

It is here, perched up on the cliff faces of the park's southern boundary, that you will find **Jedson's Wilderness Camp**, one of the region's most rustic and tranquil camps. While game drives are possible, the road network is thankfully scant, hence the camp specialises in walking safaris through the hills and valleys of the region in search of elephant, buffalo and a variety of other plains game species. Although sightings are not regular, on foot every experience is immensely rewarding and it is a haven for bird-watchers, particularly the raptors. Once the day is done, it is a perfect site to view the sweeping vistas across the plains beyond, or sip sundowners from a magnificent vantage deck a short distance away.

VICTORIA FALLS AND
ZAMBEZI NATIONAL PARKS

The Victoria Falls National Park covers a mere 23.5 square kilometres and protects the immediate rainforest and fringing riverine forest of the Victoria Falls. It is Zimbabwe's smallest but because of the waterfall, it is also far and away the busiest national park. Visitors will most often confine their time here to viewing the waterfall from the various vantage points and strolling beneath the ever-present mist of spray that filters through the rainforest.

Lying opposite the Mosi-oa-Tunya National Park in Zambia, a few kilometres upstream of the waterfall, is the gate to the Zambezi National Park, another small, protected area that stretches for approximately 40 kilometres along the river bank. Once included with the Victoria Falls National Park as a single park, the two were split in 1979 to accommodate expansion of Victoria Falls town along the riverfront. It is best suited for day trips and walking safaris, and while wildlife sightings are not prolific, elephant, hippo and a variety of plains game species are commonly seen during the winter months. The mix of woodland, riverine forest and the river system provides for outstanding birding. The park has a number of designated riverside campsites, which can be booked at the park gates, and many of the canoeing trips that are so popular with visitors begin from various put-in points in the park.

In Zambia

KAFUE NATIONAL PARK

Kafue is Zambia's largest and oldest national park (proclaimed in 1950). It covers 22 480 square kilometres and incorporates a substantial section of the Kafue River, one of the sub-continent's most impressive river systems. Kafue was once prized as one of Africa's 'big five' national parks. A period of neglect followed during the 1980s and 1990s, as it became the country's forgotten wilderness. A combination of falling tourist numbers, poor management and little development saw Kafue endure a sad chapter of rampant poaching, unprofessional trophy hunting and excessive and uncontrolled burning. Its impressive size has no doubt been the primary factor that has spared it from a worse fate. Under the management of various national wildlife authorities, the de facto running of the park has been in the hands of a few private operators, and initiatives carried out by WWF (World Wide Fund for Nature) and other international NGOs. It was a best case scenario under the circumstances and while it stemmed the tide of decay, was not sufficient to ensure full protection of the wildlife and the land.

However, there is welcome news for Kafue and those in search of less trodden tracts of wild Africa, as the park's fortunes have changed. Wilderness Safaris (WS), one of Africa's largest and most reputable ecotourism operators, has recently completed a substantial investment into Kafue and Zambia. They have established five small, rustic bush camps that will create a 'northern circuit' in the park. **Lunga River Camp** and **Nkondo Trails Camp** are situated on the banks of the Lunga River, in northeastern Kafue. **Busanga Bush Camp**, **Kapinga Bush Camp** and **Shumba Bush Camp** are all in the region of the Busanga Plains.

It is the Busanga Plains in the far northwestern corner of the park that hold Kafue's most fascinating treasures. There is an inspiring mystery about the place, an aura of ancient times suggesting that this vast, seasonal wetland was once home to an abundance of wildlife that roamed an everchanging landscape. The system covers approximately 800 square kilometres, only a snip of the park's overall size, but in many ways it is the barometer for the general state of Kafue. It comprises a patchwork of vast alluvial floodplains and grassy dambos, interspersed with countless termite mounds, fringed by pockets of dry forest established on the outlying higher ground. The network of floodplains and dambos is fed by the Busanga Swamp, a small narrow strip of papyrus-dominated marshland of 50 square kilometres fed in turn by the Lufupa River, which has its source in the northwestern regions of Zambia.

Although the wildlife has suffered heavily at the hands of poachers, the plains still offer a great safari option, and with the promise of regular eco-tourism and active and effective management, this is only going to improve as animal populations revive. Besides the presence of all the large predators, including excellent cheetah and leopard sightings, of particular interest are the 21 species of antelope that occur within its boundaries. Some of these are seldom seen anywhere else in Southern Africa: the Kafue lechwe, a subspecies of red lechwe, and puku, which are commonly seen in large herds alongside the channels that criss-cross the plains. Others of interest include sitatunga, roan antelope, oribi, Defassa's waterbuck and Lichtenstein's hartebeest.

All the larger herbivores are also present but it will take time for buffalo, elephant and hippo numbers to return to the levels last seen in the mid 1900s. The last black rhino were shot in the 1980s. The birdlife in the park is abundant, with a species count of over 500. This includes one of the continent's remaining breeding strongholds for wattled cranes and species such as Fülleborn's longclaw, Denham's bustard and the endemic Chaplin's barbet.

MOSI-OA-TUNYA NATIONAL PARK

Zambia's smallest national park, covering a mere 66 square kilometres along the Upper Zambezi River, lies on Livingstone's doorstep and includes the Zambian side of the Victoria Falls.

All visitors to the waterfall will enter the park at the Makuni Craft Village entrance, but to get some sense of the layout, it's best to take a day trip or walking safari through the mix of riverine forest and mopane woodland upstream of the waterfall. While the wildlife is not prolific and there are no predators, the park carries Zambia's only white rhino and visitors

are likely to see other plains game species such as giraffe, zebra and a variety of antelope species. The most rewarding way to see the rhino is on foot, an option offered by most operators based in Livingstone. During the dry winter months, elephant wades the river, a sight best viewed from the deck of a sundowner cruise boat. Those interested in the history of the region may choose to visit the Old Drift Cemetery site, where the first European settlers to the region were buried.

Previous page, top: *Puku graze in the early morning mists of Kafue National Park.* **Previous page, bottom:** *After years of heavy poaching, elephant herds are building up in Kafue National Park.* **Below:** *Flocks of crowned cranes are a regular sighting on the Busanga Plains of Kafue.*

In Botswana

CHOBE NATIONAL PARK

While the Okavango Delta may be Botswana's prize wilderness treasure, Chobe is regarded as the **premier national park**. At 11 700 square kilometres, it is the country's third largest protected area, but it was the first to be declared after independence and for many it is the most diverse in terms of both terrain and species. Although moves to have the region declared a national park were mooted back in 1931, this only became a reality decades later. In an effort to curb looming environmental destruction brought on by excessive logging and hunting, the pre-independence authorities afforded protection status as a game reserve in 1960 before full national park status followed in 1967. This brought ramifications for the Serondela community, a small settlement within the park's boundaries who made a living from the timber industry. They were moved out, with the last inhabitants leaving in 1975.

Because of its size and geographical positioning, straddling various vegetation and climatic zones, Chobe has four distinct eco-systems. The riverine forest and floodplain stretch along the river in the far northeast; the Linyanti River system lies in the northwest; the Savuti Marsh in the west; and the mixed dry forest and woodlands in the central, eastern and southern regions. Within these vegetation zones roam an immense diversity of wildlife, including Africa's densest concentrations of **elephant**. The counts vary but most point to somewhere between 80 000 and 120 000 of these gracious giants using the greater Chobe area as their core home range. Decimated in most other areas by ivory poaching in the middle to late decades of the last century, the Botswana and Chobe populations were spared, while also benefiting from populations fleeing other areas. Elephant are the parks major attraction, particularly during the dry winter and spring months, when they return from their summer grazing grounds in the south and congregate in their tens of thousands along the Chobe and Linyanti riverfronts. The cat predators are also commonly seen and although wild dog sightings are uncommon, they do occur. Large herds of buffalo favour the Chobe riverfront and, often with lions in tow, move back and forth between the mainland and the islands. Other highlights while driving the riverfront include puku and Chobe bushbuck, two localised antelope species found nowhere else in the region; and hippo, found on almost every riverbend and sandbar.

It must also be said that the Chobe riverfront is the most 'commercial' and crowded region in Botswana, particularly during the peak game-viewing months. Large numbers of day trip vehicles enter the park from the Kasane side, making the strip between the gate and Serondela something of a crush. For the lodge seekers, the best way to avoid this is to head for one of the lodges situated on private sites. **Chobe Chilwero**, the region's premier luxury lodge, is located on a hillside verging the park's Kasane gate end. Time here is a treat in every sense and it is the ultimate Chobe experience for those without budgetary constraints. The best mid-level option is the **Chobe Game Lodge**, a well-known landmark along the banks of the Chobe River. While it is large and more akin to a hotel, the privacy and positioning more than compensate.

Self-drive travellers need to be aware that a 4x4 vehicle is essential, as much of the park is covered in deep sand and during the summer rains, the soil patches become extremely muddy. It is also imperative to pre-book dates and sites for camping in the designated public camp sites. For those heading south, the Savuti Marsh beckons. Savuti became world renowned through various film makers who managed to capture the unfolding wildlife drama when the Savuti Channel dried up in 1981. During the dry winter months, the pans and pumped water holes offer magnificent viewing, especially for elephant and lion sightings. In the summer months, the action moves mostly onto the fertile Savuti Marsh, where large herds of zebra and wildebeest, among many other species, congregate to graze on the sweeter grasses brought on by the rains.

Because of the game viewing and the testing conditions, the route between Chobe and Maun via the Savuti Marsh is an extremely popular one. Drivers must be self-sufficient with all supplies and fuel, as there is nowhere to stock up en route.

IMPALILA ISLAND LODGE

The confluence of the Zambezi and Chobe rivers can be a busy place. This is especially so during the dry season months, when the lure of the Chobe riverfront's elephant population sees the lodges and hotels at or near peak occupancy. The unique geographical feature of the area also draws visitors: four countries, Namibia, Zambia, Zimbabwe and Botswana have international boundaries that converge at one point. For those seeking a tranquil island option hidden from the more hectic stretches of water, **Impalila Island Lodge** should be your choice.

Tucked away in Namibian waters on a private island, amongst a maze of smaller channels, this 16-bed luxury lodge offers all the comforts and treats of an island hideaway. The setting is superb with all the opportunities to visit Chobe National Park and Victoria Falls, and the waterways offer excellent fly and lure fishing on a catch and release basis, and exceptional birding and river cruises.

For access, they have their own airstrip, or contact the lodge office in Kasane for a boat transfer from the Chobe riverfront.

Above: *Dinner on the lawns of Chobe Chilwero.* **Below:** *Fly-fishing for tiger fish on the Zambezi River.*
Opposite: *Buffalo are commonly seen along the banks of the Chobe River.*

Be guided

While location, comfort levels and the quality of attractions all go to make for a memorable safari, your guide will make the difference between an ordinary safari and one of a lifetime. Because all three countries have well-established safari industries, there are a host of quality and experienced guides. Ask friends who have travelled to the region, or your agent, to recommend a guide who will fit your particular interests and type of safari.

OBERT MAFUKA »

The most solid of reputations are those built over time and there are few guides in Zimbabwe today who have done more than Obert Mafuka. Covering every national park and reserve, Obert has spent 41 years in the bush, and in the process he has gained immense respect from his peers for his bush craft, tracking skills and general knowledge.

Much of his early career was spent with the various national parks authorities, where his father also worked, and he has two brothers who have become parks wardens. Obert then did a spell as a professional hunter; more recently he has been a professional photographic guide with a number of operators. For the last six years he has been a head guide with Wilderness Safaris in the Linkwasha and Makalolo Concessions in Hwange.

Obert is also a renowned storyteller, keeping his guests and peers spellbound with his humorous and animated tales of African folklore and his bush experiences. He has one remaining wish, to be able to impart his knowledge and experiences to the schoolchildren of Zimbabwe.

« PETER GAVA

On first meeting Peter Gava, you immediately sense that you are in the company of a learned man. Engaging and extremely well spoken, it is not surprising to find that much of his 25-year career in wildlife management and guiding has included college and university studies, training, writing and working on various ecological research teams.

Born and brought up in Bulawayo, he's worked at a school bordering Chiriba National Park, where he taught environmental sciences. Peter came into contact with Dr Colin Craig and Dr Deborah Gibson, ecologists at the park, who soon became his mentors. They encouraged him to change careers, which he duly did. Peter started as a research assistant, before heading to a wildlife college in Tanzania. He also completed tourism and business diplomas before joining Hwange National Park.

Peter joined CC Africa in 1999 and is now the Operations Manager and Head Ranger for the camps in their Matetsi concession in Zimbabwe. In his spare time, he is working towards a BSc degree in geography and environmental studies.

CHIKA KACHANA »

Chika Kachana was born and brought up in Mabele Village, close to the shores of the Chobe River. As a young boy, he recalls never wanting to do anything else with his adult life other than get to know the entire river system and the adjoining Chobe National Park. So it was that after school, he signed up with the Department of Wildlife and National Parks, Botswana's wildlife authority, to undergo their guide-training course.

He now has nine years' experience as a full professional guide, all of them in the Chobe area, and the last five with Sanctuary Lodges, based at Chobe Chilwero. For Chika, it is the Chobe River and its waterfront that make the park so special. He loves nothing more than doing the afternoon river cruises during the peak elephant-viewing period from July to October.

When away from the bush, Chika is consumed by his other passion in life – soccer. He is a senior official for Chobe's major league club, and spent five years playing for the team.

« BARRY STYLE

Barry, along with his brother Rob, runs Buffalo Range Safaris, one of Zimbabwe's oldest and best-known hunting operations. Their father, Clive Style, started the company in 1973 and established its base on Buffalo Range ranch in the Chiredzi District of the Lowveld.

After qualifying as professional hunters, Rob in 1982 and Barry in 1994, they spent most of their early years hunting on the family ranch before extending their operation in the late 1990s to include concessions in the Zambezi Valley and Matetsi, where they now conduct most of their hunts. Barry also hunts in Cameroon and the Central African Republic. They specialise in tailor-made safaris for dangerous and plains game species.

During the mid 1990s, they were instrumental in establishing the Chiredzi River Conservancy, one of Zimbabwe's largest. Despite being affected by the land invasions that have impacted so adversely on Zimbabwe, it still holds a healthy population of black rhino and various other plains game species, and is the place where the Styles have their own hunting lodge.

INNOCENT CHIGAMA »

Born and brought up in Harare, Innocent started his working life in tourism in Kariba. After a spell working in hotels, he was persuaded by a friend to join the staff at the legendary Explorers pub in Victoria Falls. This was in the early nineties, an exciting time as the town and the Zambezi River fast gained a worldwide reputation as the place to be for white water sports. Explorers was always packed and for Innocent, being surrounded by rafting guides, canoeists and hordes of visiting adrenaline junkies proved inspirational. So much so that he took to the water – after completing his 1 000 hours as a trainee, he qualified as a full, professional river guide.

Innocent now has 11 years of guiding and has earned a reputation as one of the most patient and safety-conscious guides on the Zambezi. He does most of his trips on the Upper Zambezi, half-day trips, full day trips or his favourite option, spending a week camping out along the river.

« CLEMENT 'POTATO' CHISANGWA

Braving the waters of the Zambezi River on a daily basis is demanding. Most river guides succumb to the stresses and move on after a few years, but one who has outlasted his peers is Clement Chisangwa, otherwise known as 'Potato' to his many friends and guests.

Born in Livingstone, he grew up with the river as an integral part of his life. After school, he followed the advice of a close friend and joined a rafting company as a trainee guide. That was in 1995 and after learning the waters, he joined Bundu Adventures in 1998, where he has been ever since. He is now their head guide – after 11 years of guiding, Potato has successfully taken over 3 000 thrill seekers through the gorge.

For Potato, being a successful rafting guide is all about reading the mood of his guests and keeping them entertained without ever placing the raft or their lives in danger. He loves the low water season best, particularly rapid 7, which he says is 'the most technical, long and exciting ride of them all'. He is also involved in training the younger guides and plans to study tourism management once he packs his oars away.

The scene from the deck at Jedsons Wilderness Camp in Chizarira.

WILDLIFE
WONDERS

Previous spread:
*Bateleurs are regularly
seen throughout
northern Botswana,
Hwange and the
Zambezi Valley.*
Left: *While lion are
still seen regularly
in Hwange, their
numbers have declined
over the last two
decades because of
unsustainable hunting
practices.*
Next spread:
*During the summer
months, wildebeest
gather in large
herds on the open
plains of Hwange.*

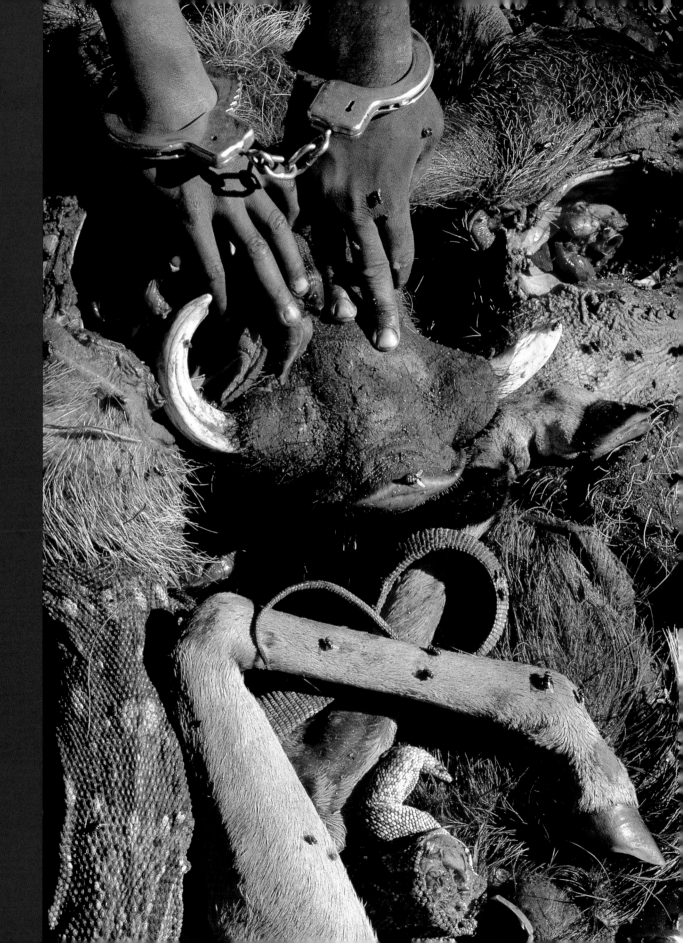

Under threat

Of the three countries, Botswana has the best record with regard to its conservation history and present policies. Its land utilisation acts, for instance, are used as examples elsewhere in Africa. Other than rhinoceros, the population status of most species found within the national parks is healthy. In contrast, Zambian wilderness areas have suffered general neglect for decades. A combination of insufficient funding, an underdeveloped infrastructure and a lack of will on the part of the authorities have been the main reasons. Maintenance and protection have been carried out mainly by private tourism operators and NGOs. This situation is improving as tourism investment picks up. In the case of Zimbabwe, prior to the land invasions in 2000, the country had a solid conservation and wildlife management reputation. Since 2000, most of

this has fallen away, along with the general demise of the economy and the country. There are now serious funding and manpower concerns, and poaching and vegetation destruction associated with new landowners have increased substantially in certain areas, particularly on the private wildlife conservancies.

Because of higher tourism levels and better infrastructure development, the regions covered in this book are generally well looked after, although there are various specific threats worth highlighting:

- **Habitat degradation** is a serious environmental concern in western Zambia, along the Zambezi River, around the edges of Hwange National Park and in the Dambwa Forest Reserve outside Livingstone. Caused by growing human pressure, this takes the form of slash and burn agricultural practices, forest

Opposite: *A meat poacher's haul.* **Below:** *Annually, uncontrolled burning takes place across the Caprivi Strip.*

clearing by charcoal cutters and commercial loggers, and overgrazing by domestic livestock.

- Although not as severe in other parts of Zambia and Zimbabwe, **poaching** is still a concern around Kafue National Park, particularly in the north and west; in Hwange National Park, particularly along the southern boundary, and in the Matetsi region.

- Annually, **uncontrolled burning** takes place across the Caprivi Strip in Namibia, with these fires often spreading into the Chobe National Park and along the Linyanti System. Excessive burning leads to vegetation loss and desertification. Fires are also a problem in western Zambia.

- There are two **major dams** on the Zambezi and one on the Kafue, its major tributary, but more are possibly to come. Zambia and Zimbabwe have signed preliminary agreements and first phase feasibility studies have been conducted on a potential site, known as the Batoka Gorge Dam site, some 60 kilometres downstream of Victoria Falls. If allowed to go ahead, a third dam will have environmental consequences. Dams reduce silt deposition and nutrient availability, alter erosion patterns and result in soil salinisation and introduction of invasive species. The dam would also in all likelihood kill the vibrant eco-tourism industry that is the lifeblood of both Livingstone and Victoria Falls town.

- With the high number of visitors, several localities within the region are beginning to suffer from **overutilisation**. The riverfront section of the Chobe National Park becomes congested with game drive vehicles in the high season; helicopters and micro lights over Victoria Falls are creating high levels of noise pollution and are a disturbance to a variety of raptor species. Visitors trampling the area immediately around the waterfall cause drainage and erosion problems as well as allowing invasive species such as *Lantana camara* to flourish.

- There should also be concern at the number of **proposed developments** in the immediate vicinity of the waterfall, on both sides of the river. There are strong indications that Mosi-oa-Tunya National Park is about to be carved up into a number of new concessions for hotels and lodges, and plans are afoot to build a golf course at the junction of the Maramba and Zambezi rivers. On the Zimbabwean side, more hotel and lodge sites are to be allocated along the river.

- Unsustainable **trophy hunting** in the private concessions surrounding Hwange and Matetsi has impacted on the lion populations to the extent that a moratorium has been declared. In the future, if hunting is allowed to continue without proper supervision, this population will be under serious threat.

Opposite: *While cheetah are not adept at climbing trees, cubs do clamber about low branches and fallen trunks.*
Below left: *Sable antelope, one of Africa's rarest species, can be seen in Hwange and Chobe.* **Below right:** *A chacma baboon.*

Science and conservation

While by no means complete, below is a list of private and quasi-government bodies involved in research, education and general conservation work within the regions covered by this book. Their efforts are crucial to maintaining the wilderness regions and their biodiversity. Many of these organisations rely on private funding, donations and volunteer work to carry out their objectives. Anyone wishing to become involved, either as a volunteer, or to assist with financial aid, may contact them.

ZIMBABWE

Hwange Lion Research Project – In operation since 1999, this project is involved in assessing hunting impacts on lion populations, as well as research on general lion behaviour, ranges and population size in Hwange National Park. E-mail: andrew.loveridge@zoology.oxford.ac.uk

Painted Hunting Dog Research Project – This is a wild dog conservation and management project conducted in Hwange National Park. The project includes scientific research on range and behaviour of wild dogs, and outreach community education programmes. E-mail: phdrpete@mweb.co.zw

ZAMBIA

Wildlife Environmental Conservation Society of Zambia (Livingstone Branch) – This national body operates as an action group to raise awareness and promote the wise use of natural resources. Tel: +260 97 750493, e-mail: mikemusgravezw@yahoo.co.uk

The Zambian Ornithological Society – They work with Birdlife International, focusing on important bird areas and biodiversity protection in general. E-mail: zos@zamnet.zm

BOTSWANA

The Chobe Wildlife Trust – This independent organisation was created to assist with conservation, research and education, focused on Chobe National Park and northern Botswana. Tel: +267 6250312, e-mail: cwt@info.bw

Large Carnivore Research – Based in Kasane, this project monitors and collects data on all large predators in the Chobe and Caprivi Strip regions. Tel: +267 6252385, e-mail: gmahupeleng@botsnet.bw

GOSIAME MAHUPELENG

Growing up in the village of Kachikau on the banks of the Chobe River afforded Gosiame Mahupeleng a good start in life. Spending his youth in the region's rich wildlife heritage was a joy and, in his later years, the inspiration to follow a career in the scientific and research world. After his schooling, he went on to gain a degree in Biological and Environmental Science at the University of Botswana, and then a Masters degree in Natural Resources Management from the Agricultural University of Norway.

After a stint with the Department of Wildlife and National Parks in Botswana, he joined the African Wildlife Foundation (AWF), a USA based conservation organisation, as a wildlife biologist. Gosiame is presently in his third year of an extensive large carnivore research project covering the Chobe and Linyanti regions of northern Botswana. His work entails population estimates and constructing distribution maps for lion, leopard, spotted hyena, wild dog and jackal; as well as carrying out monitoring and education programmes related to human-carnivore conflict in the study area.

For Gosiame, the work will ensure that we understand the exact status of the region's carnivores, promoting the concept of equitable resource utilisation between the tourism industry and the local communities in the Chobe district. He plans to use this project as the basis for his doctorate.

Opposite: *The Chobe and Zambezi rivers still carry large populations of hippo.* **Below:** *A mother cheetah and sub-adult in Hwange.*

Green-backed herons are found along all the river systems throughout the region.

Puku are an antelope species associated with the floodplains of northern Kafue National Park.

Opposite: *Pangolin are an extremely rare sighting in the wild.*
Left, top: *A black-backed jackal sniffs the morning air.*
Left: *African purple swamp hen are seen along the backwaters and lagoons of the major river systems in the region.*

OUT OF THE WAY

Previous spread: *Low-flying along the banks of Lake Kariba.* **Above:** *Mana Pools National Park.*

Although regarded as being somewhat out of the way, it is extremely worthwhile considering one or more of these destinations as core components to a safari, or at the very least, as add-ons. For some you will be able to travel by road, but you will need to be self-sufficient during the trip, particularly with regard to water and fuel supplies. Villages encountered along the way have rudimentary supplies of basic foodstuffs and drink, but often not much else. If your final destination is a recognised lodge or camp, then you will be well catered for upon arrival. Attending the Kuomboka in Barotseland will entail a fair amount of prior planning and constant checking as to whether the ceremony will take place or not.

The Kuomboka

Barotseland is the home of the **Lozi people** in Zambia. Covering most of the area known today as the Western Province, these ancestral lands include the vast floodplains of the Upper Zambezi River. In the seventeenth century, the Lozi began settling in the luxuriant and fertile network of waterways and islands dominating this section of the Zambezi, after moving south from Central Africa. Known to the Lozi as the Ngulu-Ta-Toya, it was here that they established an enduring and powerful kingdom that today still continues to uphold many of the rich traditions central to their customary life.

The most important and spectacular event in their cultural calendar is the **Kuomboka**, a ceremony celebrating the annual relocation of the Lozi king, the *Litunga*, from his summer floodplain palace, Lealui, to his winter mainland palace, Limulunga. For eight months of the year the Lozi inhabit the lush wetlands, planting and harvesting crops, fishing and grazing their livestock. With the onset of the summer rains, water levels begin rising and by March, the annual floodwaters of the greater Zambezi catchment area have risen to levels that force the *Litunga*, his royal household and the many villagers to leave the floodplains for higher ground. The word *kuomboka* literally means 'to move away from water'.

Although the ceremony is traditionally a Lozi one and began hundreds of years ago out of necessity, it has more recently become a celebration for all who live in western Zambia. Dictated by the floodwaters, the exact timing of the great move is the decision of the *Litunga* and takes place in a flotilla of craft headed by the royal barge, or the *Nalikwanda*, which carries the *Litunga*, his family and guests. Two other barges and any number of vessels, ranging from motorised boats to flimsy wooden dugout canoes, all laden to the hilt, follow them.

Page 131: *The barge that carries the king during the Kuomboka ceremony is called the Nalikwanda.* **Previous spread:** *The Nalikwanda arrives at Limulunga where the Lozi king will spend the winter months.* **Above:** *The paddlers of the Nalikwanda do some showboating before the king disembarks.* **Opposite:** *Musical fanfare is an integral part of the Kuomboka ceremony.*

Forty-eight hours before the event, the king's paddlers are 'called' to the island of Lealui by the palace drummers, who bring out 200-year-old royal war drums and engage in a night of rousing drumming. The echoes sound and word spreads quickly as participants gather at the mainland town of Mongu and find their way to Lealui. On the day of the ceremony there is much **fanfare** as military-style bands and local musicians keep the crowds entertained as they wait for the Litunga to emerge from the palace. His imminent appearance is preceded by a long line of royal attendants who snake their way through the throng, each carrying an article of luggage and his personal belongings to be loaded for the move. He boards the Nalikwanda to delighted cheers from the villagers and the royal drummers begin thumping the rhythm that will keep the paddlers going for the next six to eight hours. After a ritualistic farewell passage around the island, the barges set off across the grassy floodplains, followed by the fleet of dugouts, long boats and small rowing boats who constantly jostle for position as they try to be closest to the royal barge.

The undoubted highlight of the ceremony is the eventual arrival of the barges and the flotsam of following craft at Limulunga. The reception that the flotilla receives from the approximately 15 000 people who gather there is nothing short of rapturous. The paddlers of the royal barge draw inspiration from the crowd's approval and as the royal drummers up the tempo to a thunderous beat, they reciprocate the welcome with a thrilling finale of showboating and fervent rhythmic paddling that draws an even more frenzied response as they perform up and down the final stretch of water. It is only after the sun has fallen that the king disembarks to join his subjects in festivities that proceed well into the night.

An element of Zambia's **colonial past** makes its appearance at the ceremony. When the Litunga leaves Lealui he is dressed in ordinary clothing, but when he disembarks at Limulunga, he does so in a full British admiral's tunic with silver buttons, brass braiding and ostrich-plumed headgear to boot. Barotseland was given official British protectorate status in 1900, to safeguard it from the marauding Matabele people; this in exchange for various mineral and land rights granted earlier to Cecil John Rhodes. The (then) Lozi king, Lewanika, was presented with an admiral's uniform in 1902 by King Edward VII, in honour of the treaties signed by the parties, and so began the tradition of the Litunga's dress code.

What is so inspiring about the Kuomboka is that it is still carried out in the most venerable of ways, with an immense sense of pride and honour for the self-respecting tradition of the Lozi people and their king. The spectacle is enhanced by the extremely tangible and obvious level of excitement and enjoyment experienced by the thousands and thousands of citizens of Barotseland who willingly flock from all parts of the province to participate in some way. **To follow the ceremony**, contact the Zambian tourism authority in Livingstone (+260 3 321404/5) or any local tour operator to check for dates before heading for the town of Mongu.

Mana Pools

Somewhat further out of the way than the other options covered in this section, **Mana Pools** most certainly deserves mention by virtue of its magnificent setting, superb game viewing and legendary canoe trails. For the many regular visitors to Zimbabwe, this park and stretch of the river is the **gem of the Zambezi Valley**.

Covering an old floodplain area where the river once meandered widely, the park's most distinctive features are the gigantic ana trees and Natal mahogany that dominate the ribbon of riverine woodland running the length of this section of the southern bank of the Zambezi. The hallmark sighting, commonly seen during the drier months, must surely be giant elephant bulls stretching up, balanced on their hind legs to reach and shake fresh pods from the ana trees. The general game viewing is outstanding with all the predators to be found, including regular wild dog sightings. The drier acacia woodland away from the river carries many herbivore species, and for the birders there is plenty to spot.

There are two top-end lodge options, **Ruckomechi** in the west and **Chikwenya** in the east, both with wonderful riverfront settings, but the most thrilling Mana experience is by canoe. Start at Ruckomechi and spend the next few days paddling your way downstream towards Chikwenya. Night-time is spent camping out on the banks, and mornings are often taken up with walks and exciting encounters with wildlife on foot.

There are public campsites at Mana, which can be booked through the Zimbabwean wildlife authorities.

Kariba and Matusadona

Once a bustling centre for Zimbabwean and foreign visitors alike, Kariba (see 'A Region of Rivers' page 52) and Matusadona National Park on the southern shores have fallen on hard times over the last few years. The political and economic troubles of Zimbabwe have taken their toll, with many lodges and hotels closing down and others battling merely to stay in business. Since the construction of the dam and the build-up of the lake in the early 1960s, Kariba has always been about houseboats and cruising these vast waters.

During the 1980s and 1990s, Kariba cruises launched from either Binga or Kariba town were legendary for the fantastic shoreline sightings of wildlife, the tigerfish and bream fishing, and the stunning sunsets. And Matusadona is all about walking. It's a great park to track black rhinoceros on foot, and the birdlife along the shoreline is fantastic. These options are still available but, because of the fluid nature of the political climate, it is best to contact one of the operators listed in the travel directory for an update.

Previous spread: *Close-up views of elephant are a highlight of the Mana Pools canoe trail.*
Opposite: *On foot in the Mana Pools National Park.* **Below:** *A characteristic Kariba sunset.*

the
LIFE & SOUL

There is a truism in the safari world that is most certainly worth repeating here: meeting the local people on your trip is one of the most rewarding aspects. The Victoria Falls region has a **remarkable diversity** of people to meet. Besides those who have historically lived here, many more groups are represented because of the tourism industry. Over the decades they have been drawn by the opportunities: as guides, working in the hotels and lodges or setting up their own businesses selling arts, crafts, curios and supplies to tourists and the industry.

For those who enjoy the song and dance aspects of cultural life, seek out the Makishi dancers in Victoria Falls town. *Makishi* means 'a masquerade' and the elaborate costumes worn by the dancers are totems belonging to the Luvale people, who have a cultural heritage rich in spiritualism and symbolism. The craft and curio markets, local bars and eating houses are also great places to meet people and immerse yourself in the cultural traditions of the locals. You will always be welcomed and treated with courtesy and respect.

Previous spread: *A Chobe fisherman heads out in the early morning to check his nets.*
Left, top: *A selection of artifacts made by local craftsmen.*
Left: *Mopane worms, a favourite amongst rural folk of the region, for sale in a Zimbabwean market.*
Opposite: *Chickens roost in Songwe Village.*

Who's who in Zimbabwe?

Over 98 per cent of Zimbabwe's population comprises Bantu-speaking groups, with two ethnic groups, the Shona and Ndebele, dominating the population makeup.

THE SHONA

Almost 75 per cent of Zimbabwe's people are **Shona-speaking** and traditionally come from the central and eastern regions of the country. They comprise six main ethnic groups: Rozwi, Karanga, Zesuru, Manyika, Ndau and Korekore. The Shona groups are all descendants of Bantu-speaking peoples who migrated centuries earlier from the Great Lakes region of East Africa, and from West Africa before that. Based on language dialects and different cultural practices, there are over 65 sub-groupings of the Shona.

THE NDEBELE

Of the minority groups, the **Ndebele** are the largest, comprising approximately 16 per cent of the population. Known as the Matabele in colonial times, their language is S'Ndebele. The Ndebele are more recent arrivals, having settled in southwestern Zimbabwe in the early 1800s. Once part of the Zulu nation in South Africa, they followed their great leader, Mzilikazi, who broke away after various altercations with the (then) Zulu king Shaka.

OTHER GROUPS

The **Kalanga**, a group closely related to the Ndebele, comprise about three per cent of the population and live along the extreme western border with Botswana. The **Tonga** have traditionally lived along the Zambezi Valley, and where Kariba Dam is situated. The **Venda** and **Shangaan** are from southern Zimbabwe and the **Chewa** from northeastern Zimbabwe. People of **Asian** and **European** extraction comprise less than one per cent of the population.

THE LANGUAGES

While **English** is the official language, **Shona** and **S'Ndebele** are regarded as national languages. Over 80 per cent of the population speak Shona in Zimbabwe, and regionally the language is spoken by over seven million people (including Mozambique and Zambia). Shona is a Bantu language belonging to the Niger-Congo family. S'Ndebele is spoken by approximately 20 per cent of the population and comes from the Nguni group of Bantu languages.

Who's who in Zambia?

Over 95 per cent of Zambia's population has **Bantu origins**. They can broadly be divided into one of seven main ethnolinguistic groups. Amongst these main groups, there are over 70 different language dialects and cultural differences. Most of the ethnic groups are small, with only two comprising more than 10 per cent of the population. While still comprising approximately one per cent of the population, the country has a growing **European** and **Asian** population.

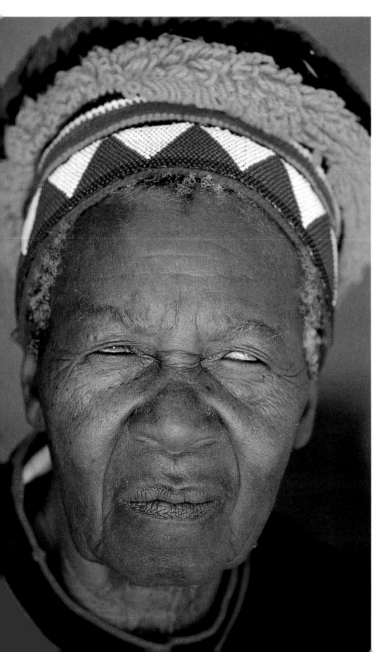

THE SEVEN GROUPS

Bemba – Comprising almost 20 per cent of the population, they are the largest group and live mostly along the Copperbelt and in the northeast.

Chewa – Also known as the Nyanja, they are the second largest group and make up just over 10 per cent of the population. The Chewa traditionally live in the eastern regions, along the border with Malawi.

Tonga – They comprise approximately eight per cent of the population, and traditionally live along the Zambezi Valley.

Lozi –They came from the north and west and settled in western Zambia, amongst the floodplains of the Zambezi River. A smaller group, the Makololo came from the south and were absorbed as part of the Lozi.

Lunda – Originally from further north and descendants of the Mwata Yamvo empire that once ruled over most of the present-day Democratic Republic of Congo, they settled in the north west of Zambia.

Luvale – One of the smaller groups, they came from the north and settled in the northeast of the country, around Lake Tanganyika.

Kaonde – They settled along the northern border with Zaire, particularly in the Copperbelt region.

THE LANGUAGES

English is the **official language** of Zambia but there are over 70 local languages and dialects. Of these, the languages of the seven major groups listed above are the most widely spoken.

Left: *Over 95 per cent of Zambia's population can be broadly divided into seven main ethno-linguistic groups.*
Opposite: *This eccentric man from Sesheke claims to be the town's local electrician.*

Who's who in Botswana?

Citizens of Botswana are collectively referred to as Batswana (plural form) or Motswana (singular form), and can be grouped into two broad categories: Setswana-speaking or Tswana; and non-Setswana-speaking. Over 60 per cent of the population traces its heritage to one of the Setswana-speaking groups. Despite Botswana's recognition as a leading example of democracy in Africa, where human rights are guaranteed, the Constitution of the country recognises only eight ethnic groups for permanent representation in the House of Chiefs. These are the Bakgatla, Bakwena, Bamalete, Bamangwato, Bangwaketse, Barolong, Batawana and Batlokwa groups.

THE TSWANA GROUPS

The biggest of these groups, the **Bangwato**, **Bakwena** and **Bangwaketse**, are culturally related and take their names from descendants of King Mogale, who ruled the southern regions of present-day Botswana and parts of western South Africa, over 400 years ago. The Bangwato, the largest of these groups, settled in the central regions around Serowe. The Bangwaketse and Bakwena are found in the southern and eastern regions. The **Batawana** are a breakaway group from the Bangwato, who settled further north around the southern edges of the Okavango.

The other major Tswana groups are: the **Bakgatla**, **Batlokwa** and **Barolong**, from the southeastern regions; the **Bahurutshe** in the central regions; the **Babirwa** in the east; and the **Bakgalagadi**, one of the oldest groups, comprising a number of smaller ethnic groups, in the central and southern regions of the Kalahari.

THE NON-TSWANA GROUPS

There are several non-Tswana ethnic groups who constitute an important segment of the population. They are believed to have come into Botswana from the north and northwest.

The **Bakalanga** comprise various smaller ethnic groups who together make up the largest of the non-Setswana-speaking groups and one of the largest individual groups in the country. Arriving from present-day Zimbabwe, they settled in the eastern regions of the country. The **Bamalete** are found in the southeastern regions, along the border with South Africa. The **Bayei** and **Mbukushu** came from the north and settled around the Okavango Delta. The **Basubiya** settled in the northern regions along the Chobe River. The **Basarwa** or San, the earliest inhabitants, still survive in small extended family groups throughout the central Kalahari and in the west. The **Baherero** are the most recent immigrants, arriving in the early 1900s after fleeing German occupation in Namibia. They settled along the western and southern edges of the Okavango Delta. People of European and Asian descent began arriving in the early decades of the nineteenth century, settling mostly in the urban areas and the Okavango Delta. The Ghanzi district was settled by a group of Afrikaans-speaking people who moved up from South Africa.

THE LANGUAGE

While **English** is the official language, **Setswana** is the national language of Botswana, spoken by almost 90 per cent of its citizens. Setswana is also one of South Africa's national languages, spoken by over four million people in Southern Africa. Setswana is a Bantu language belonging to the Niger-Congo language family and is closely related to North and South Sotho. It first appeared in its written form in the early 1800s, in Bible translations done by various missionaries, including Dr Robert Moffatt.

There are over 20 other languages spoken in the country, mostly by the non-Setswana-speaking groups. Sekalanga, spoken by the Bakalanga, is the most commonly used of these languages. English is spoken throughout the urban areas and within all tourist facilities, but is not common in most rural areas.

Opposite: Botswana is well known for its high-quality baskets, woven from strips of palm leaf.

Above: A grass cutter from the Chobe District sorts grass into bundles for the market.

Page 148: The road to Livingstone.

travel
DIRECTORY

Travel advisory

LOCAL TIME AND DIALLING CODES

Zimbabwe, Zambia and Botswana use GMT (Greenwich Mean Time) plus two hours. There is no Daylight Saving Time. International dialling codes: Zimbabwe +263, Zambia +260, Botswana +267 followed by area codes and telephone number. Outgoing dialling codes are 00 from all three countries.

CLIMATE AND WHEN TO TRAVEL

The region lies within the tropics and the climate is characterised by two distinct seasons: warm summers from late September to early April, when the rains fall; and cooler, dry winters from May through to September. The average rainfall is approximately 650 millimetres in the Kasane and Victoria Falls regions, rising to over 750 millimetres as one heads north into Zambia. The mean annual temperatures are 28° C in the summer months (with highs of over 40° C) and 18° C in the winter (with lows of below 6° C, but seldom freezing).

While the region has good conditions for travelling during most of the year, the cooler and dry winter and spring months are the most comfortable. This period also offers the best game viewing, as wildlife tends to concentrate at permanent water points. December and January are also rewarding, as many of the plains game species are calving, and the best birding is from October through to early April.

HEALTH AND MEDICINE

In general, Zimbabwe, Zambia and Botswana are classed as medium- to high-risk malaria countries. Travellers must consult their local medical practitioners for advice on what malaria prophylaxis to take prior to departure. While no vaccination certificates are required to enter any of the countries, it is worth consulting your doctor about vaccinations for tetanus, polio, hepatitis A and B, typhoid, rabies and meningitis.

While the tap water in most lodges within the national parks is fit for consumption, it is not advisable to drink any tap water while in the towns or to eat uncooked foods that may have been washed in untreated water. Bottled water is readily available in all hotels, lodges and guesthouses as well as from most stores and restaurants. All three countries have doctors and western medicines are available, but it is recommended that travellers take all basic medical requirements and specific medication with them. Most safari lodges and camps have comprehensive medical aid kits on their premises. It is advisable to carry adequate travel insurance, including cover for emergency air evacuation, and to have these details with you at all times.

EMERGENCY SERVICE NUMBERS

Visitors should carry the contact details of their booking agents and ground operators with them at all times, as these numbers should be the first to be used in an emergency.

IN ZIMBABWE

Falls Medical Centre: 95 West Drive, Victoria Falls, Tel: +263 13 40529/43356
Medical Air Rescue Service (MARS): 94 West Drive, Victoria Falls, Tel: +263 13 44646/42268

IN ZAMBIA

Emergency: 999
Police: 991
Mosi-oa-Tunya Medical Centre: +260 3 324241
MedRescue 24 hours: +260 1 273302/3/4

IN BOTSWANA

Chobe Private Clinic: +267 6251555

VISAS

The visa requirements for the three countries differ widely. Generally, citizens of European Community countries, Scandinavia, USA and South Africa do not require visas for Botswana. Citizens from most European Community countries and the USA require visas for Zimbabwe and Zambia, which may be obtained at points of entry. The costs of the visas vary according to the nationality of the passport holder. All three countries most often issue 30-day visas, which can be extended to a maximum of 90 days. As these regulations may change, it is always advisable to check with your agent before travelling.

SAFETY AND SECURITY

Generally, the region is a safe place to travel, with few incidents of serious crime reported annually. Botswana is probably the safest country in Africa in which to travel. It has an unsurpassed record regarding the safety of its tourists. While serious crime is almost non-existent, petty theft may occur in the cities and major towns. Although Zimbabwe has received negative press globally for its land invasions and the civil strife related to this, tourist regions have generally remained unaffected. Travellers passing through Harare in Zimbabwe, and Lusaka in Zambia, should be extremely cautious of pickpockets and petty theft when walking in these cities.

CURRENCY AND BANKING

The international currencies of choice in the region are the US dollar, British pound and Euro. Cash is preferable, as travellers' cheques are exchanged at lower rates and some banks, tourist establishments and retail outlets will not accept them. In Botswana and Zambia, the best places to exchange money are at exchange bureaux as they usually offer the better rates. In both countries, international credit cards are accepted in lodges and hotels and many shopping outlets.

Zimbabwe has experienced severe economic conditions since 2000, which has included spells of hyperinflation and black market currency rates. Because of this, do not exchange money anywhere other than a bank or reputable tourist establishment. It is also advisable to get an update from your travel agent prior to departure on the economic situation. In Zimbabwe, many lodges, hotels and retail outlets do not accept credit cards. Kasane, Victoria Falls and Livingstone all have major banks, but expect long queues if you have to use them.

Botswana's unit of currency is the pula, Zambia's the kwacha and Zimbabwe's the Zimbabwean dollar.

ELECTRICITY

All three countries are supplied with 220–240 volts AC, although lodges in outlying areas will usually have independent power generators. Most plugs and sockets are of the British three-square-pin 13-amp format. Adaptors are available for purchase in city and town stores and for guest use in all hotels and lodges.

TRAVEL TIPS

- For those travelling by road, a *carnet de passage* for your vehicle is not a necessity. However, if you are heading further north into Tanzania and beyond, it will be necessary. When entering Zimbabwe and Zambia you will need to fill out temporary vehicle import papers and purchase local third party insurance. In Zimbabwe there is a road and carbon tax, which varies according to the size of the motor vehicle. In Zambia, you will require an Interpol Police Clearance Certificate from the country in which your vehicle is registered, and the law requires your vehicle to have strips of reflective tape on the front and rear bumpers. Get this done as soon as you enter; the fines are hefty if you are caught without them. It is also best to travel with an international driving licence. Keep these documents in your vehicle at all times, as you will be asked to produce them by traffic officials at roadblocks.

- All three countries have road traffic police forces that are active. Obey speed limits, particularly when entering and leaving urban areas, small towns and villages, as you will encounter radar trapping stations.

- Despite the presence of 'tourism police' on the streets, Victoria Falls still has a number of touts and back-street operators lurking around the town. They will offer everything from drugs and money changing to cheap excursions. Do not be taken in and do not change money – you are sure to be cheated.

- Cell phones are extremely popular throughout Africa. Starter packs and prepaid vouchers are readily available in the urban areas of Botswana and Zambia, but are far harder to come by in Zimbabwe because of the economic conditions there. If you are spending an extended period of time in these countries, consider buying a local number.

- Do not take photographs of sensitive government buildings such as residences, military barracks and airports, or of any officials in uniform. Especially in Zimbabwe, stick to taking photographs in the recognised tourism areas only.

- Because of the economic crises and hyperinflation occurring in Zimbabwe, certain retail outlets are

abusing the situation with different prices for those paying in Zimbabwe dollars versus foreign currency. Ask the price in Zimbabwe dollars first and do the cross-calculation, as US$ and SA rand prices can be as much as 50 per cent more expensive.
- Of the three international airports, it is usually substantially cheaper to fly into Livingstone than Kasane or Victoria Falls.

WANT TO READ MORE?
Botswana – The Insider's Guide by Ian Michler
The Miracle Rivers by Peter and Beverly Pickford
Hwange – Retreat of the Elephants by Nick Greaves
Zimbabwe the Beautiful by Peter Joyce
Mosi-oa-Tunya – A Handbook to the Victoria Falls edited by D.W. Phillipson
The Zambezi – River of the Gods by Jan and Fiona Teede
The Lions & Elephants of the Chobe by Bruce Aiken
Zambia – Safari in Style by David Rogers
Zimbabwe – Lonely Planet Guide
Botswana – Lonely Planet Guide
Zambia – Lonely Planet Guide
Zambia – The Bradt Travel Guide by Chris McIntyre

Contact details – Zimbabwe

TOURISM REPRESENTATIVES
Victoria Falls Publicity Association: PO Box 97, Victoria Falls or Stand 412 Parkway Drive, Victoria Falls. Tel: +263 13 44202, e-mail: vfpa@mweb.co.zw
Zimbabwe Parks and Wildlife Management Authority – Central Reservations: PO Box CY 140, Harare. Tel: +263 4 706077/8 or 707624/9, e-mail: natparks@africaonline.co.zw

TOUR AND SAFARI OPERATORS
Invent Africa: Unit A1, Westlake Square, Westlake Drive, Tokai, 7945, Cape Town, South Africa. Tel: +27 21 7011179, e-mail: reservations@ inventafrica.com, website: www.inventafrica.com
Wilderness Safaris: PO Box 288, Victoria Falls, Zimbabwe. Tel: +263 13 43371/2/3, e-mail: enquiry@wilderness.co.za, website: www.wilderness-safaris.com
Sanctuary Lodges: P/Bag 45, Maun, Botswana. Tel: +267 6862688, e-mail: southernafrica@sanctuarylodges.com, website: www.sanctuarylodges.com
Desert & Delta Safaris: PO Box 310, Maun, Botswana. Tel: +267 6861243, e-mail: ddsres@botsnet.bw, website: www.desertdelta.com

CC Africa: P/Bag X27, Benmore, 2010, Johannesburg, South Africa. Tel: +27 11 809 4300, e-mail: information@ccafrica.com, website: www.ccafrica.com

HOTELS AND LODGES
The Victoria Falls Hotel: PO Box 10, Victoria Falls. Tel: +263 13 4751/61, e-mail: reservations@tvfh.zimsun.co.zw, website: www.lhw.com
The Stanley & Livingstone: PO Box 160, Victoria Falls. Tel: +263 13 41003 / 44557, e-mail: aujanzim@zol.co.zw, website: www.stanleyandlivingstone.com
Ilala Lodge: PO Box 18, Victoria Falls. Tel: +263 13 44737/44223, e-mail: ilalazws@africaonline.co.zw, website: www.ilalalodge.com
Victoria Falls Safari Lodge: PO Box 29, Victoria Falls. Tel: +263 13 43211/2/3, e-mail: saflodge@saflodge.co.zw, website: www.vfsl.com
Lokuthula Lodges: PO Box 29, Victoria Falls. Tel: +263 13 44717/44728, e-mail: loklodge@mweb.co.zw, website: www.vfsl.com
Elephant Hills Intercontinental: PO Box 30, Victoria Falls. Tel: +263 13 44793, e-mail: reservations@ehic.zimsun.co.zw, website: www.zimsun.co.zw

Amadeus Garden Lodge: PO Box CT 288, Victoria Falls. Tel: +263 13 42261, e-mail: info@insightafrica.de, website: www.amadeusgarden.com

The Kingdom: PO Box 90, Victoria Falls. Tel: +263 13 42759, e-mail: reservations@kingdom.zim.co.zw, website: www.zimbabwesun.com

Imbabala Safari Camp: PO Box 185, Victoria Falls. Tel: +263 13 43589, mobile +263 23 296874, e-mail: whtrain@mweb.co.zw, website: www.wildhorizons.co.zw

Savanna Lodge: 68 Courtney Crescent, Victoria Falls. Tel: +263 13 42821, e-mail: savann@telcovic.co.zw, website: www.africandestinations.co.za/savanna

Shoestrings Backpackers: 12 West Drive, Victoria Falls. Tel: +263 13 40167, e-mail: sstrings@mweb.co.zw

Jedson's Wilderness Camp: PO Box 196, Victoria Falls. Tel: +263 13 44283/42229, e-mail: dvj@mweb.co.zw or untamed@telkomsa.net, website: www.untamed-africa.com

Linkwasha: (see Wilderness Safaris)

Makololo and Little Makololo: (see Wilderness Safaris)

Matetsi Water Lodge and Matetsi Safari Camp: see CC Africa

Buffalo Range Safaris (Hunting): PO Buffalo Range, Buffalo Range, Zimbabwe. Tel: +263 11 416559 or 416004, e-mail: buffalorange@zol.co.zw, website: www.buffalorangesafari.com

ADVENTURE SPORTS

Shearwater Adventures: Parkway Drive, Victoria Falls. Tel: +263 13 44471/43392/42058, e-mail: reservations@shearwater.co.zw, website: www.shearwateradventures.com

Wild Horizons: Parkway Drive, Victoria Falls. Tel: +263 13 44571/44282 or mobile +263 11 213721/209117, e-mail: info@wildhorizons.co.zw, website: www.wildhorizons.co.zw

Contact details – Zambia

TOURISM REPRESENTATIVES

Zambia National Tourism Board – Livingstone Office: PO Box 603432, Livingstone or adjacent to the Livingstone Museum. Tel: +260 3 321404/5, e-mail: zntblive@zamnet.zm, website: www.zambiatourism.com

TOUR AND SAFARI OPERATORS

Invent Africa: Unit A1, Westlake Square, Westlake Drive, Tokai, 7945, Cape Town, South Africa. Tel: +27 21 7011179, e-mail: reservations@inventafrica.com, website: www.inventafrica.com

Wilderness Safaris: PO Box 288, Victoria Falls, Zimbabwe. Tel: +263 13 43371/2/3, e-mail: enquiry@wilderness.co.za, website: www.wilderness-safaris.com

Desert & Delta Safaris: PO Box 310, Maun, Botswana. Tel: +267 6861243, e-mail: ddsres@botsnet.bw, website: www.desertdelta.com

HOTELS AND LODGES

The River Club: (see Wilderness Safaris)

Taita Falcon Lodge: PO Box 60012, Livingstone. Tel: +263 11 208387, e-mail: taita-falcon@zamnet.zm, website: www.taitafalcon.com

Songwe Village: PO Box 550, Maun, Botswana. Tel: +260 977 83053, e-mail: reservations@kwando.co.za, website: www.kwando.co.za

The Islands of Siankaba: PO Box 60845, Livingstone. Tel: +260 3 324490 or 9 7791241, e-mail: siankaba@zamnet.zm, website: siankaba.com

Jungle Junction: PO Box 61122, Livingstone. Tel: +260 3 323708, e-mail: jungle@zamnet.zm, website: www.junglejunction.info

Tongabezi & Sindabezi: Private Bag 31, Livingstone. Tel: +260 97 771488, e-mail: reservations@tongabezi.com, website: www.tongabezi.com

The Royal Livingstone & Zambezi Sun: PO Box 60151, Livingstone. Tel: +260 3 321122, e-mail: suninzam@zamnet.com or intmrk@sunint.co.za, website: www.suninternational.com

Shackletons Upper Zambezi Lodge: PO Box 7, Mwandi. Tel: +260 97 934149 or +264 81 2232378, e-mail: info@shackletons.co.za, website: www.shackletons.co.za

Maramba River Lodge: PO Box 60957, Livingstone. Tel: +260 3 324189, e-mail: maramba@zamnet.zm, website: www.maramba-zambia.com

The Waterfront: PO Box 60407, Livingstone. Tel: +260 3 320606/7, e-mail: zaminfo@safpar.com, website: www.safpar.com

Fawlty Towers: PO Box 61170, Livingstone. Tel: +260 3 323432, e-mail: ahorizon@zamnet.zm, website: www.adventure-africa.com

Sekoma Island Lodge: (see Desert & Delta Safaris)

Jollyboys: Tel: +260 3 324229, e-mail: jollyboys@zamnet.zm, website: www.backpackzambia.com

ADVENTURE SPORTS

Batoka Sky: PO Box 60733, Livingstone. Tel: +260 3 320058 or 11 409578, e-mail: freedom@zamnet.zm, website: www.batokasky.com

Bundu Adventures: PO Box 60773, Livingstone. Tel: +260 3 324407/8, e-mail: zambezi@zamnet.zm, website: www.bundu-adventures.com

African Horizons: PO Box 61170, Livingstone. Tel: +260 3 323432, e-mail: ahorizon@zamnet.zm, website: www.adventure-africa.com

AIR CHARTER

Sefofane Botswana: Tel: +267 6860778, e-mail: reservations@sefofane.bw, website: www.sefofane.com

Sefofane Zimbabwe: Tel: +263 11 212008, e-mail: reservations@sefofane.co.zw, website: www.sefofane.com

Contact details – Botswana

TOURISM REPRESENTATIVES

Department of Tourism: PO Box 66, Kasane. Tel: + 267 6250357, e-mail: tourism.kasane@gov.bw, website: www.botswanatourism.org

Department of Wildlife and National Parks: PO Box 17, Kasane. Tel: +267 650486, e-mail: dwnp@gov.bw, reservations: parks.reservations.gaborone@gov.bw

TOUR AND SAFARI OPERATORS

Invent Africa: Unit A1, Westlake Square, Westlake Drive, Tokai, 7945, Cape Town, South Africa. Tel: +27 21 7011179, e-mail: reservations@inventafrica.com, website: www.inventafrica.com

Sanctuary Lodges: P/Bag 45, Maun, Botswana. Tel: +267 6862688, e-mail: southernafrica@sanctuarylodges.com, website: www.sanctuarylodges.com

Desert & Delta Safaris: PO Box 310, Maun, Botswana. Tel: +267 6861243, e-mail: ddsres@botsnet.bw, website: www.desertdelta.com

CC Africa: P/Bag X27, Benmore, 2010, Johannesburg, South Africa. Tel: +27 11 809 4300, e-mail: information @ccafrica.com, website: www.ccafrica.com

Safari & Guide Services: Private Bag K39, Kasane, Botswana. Tel: +267 625 1754, e-mail: travel@botsnet.bw, website: www.chobetravel.com

HOTELS AND LODGES

Chobe Chilwero: (see Sanctuary Lodges)
Chobe Game Lodge: (see Desert & Delta Safaris)
Impalila Island Lodge: PO Box 55, Kasane. Tel: +267 71303418 or +27 11 7067207, e-mail: info@islandsinafrica.com, website: www.islandsinafrica.com
The Garden Lodge: Private Bag K48, Kasane. Tel: +267 6250051 or mobile: +267 71304150, e-mail: gabi@botsnet.bw, website: www.thegardenlodge.com

Chobe Marina Lodge: Private Bag K83, Kasane. Tel: +267 6252221, e-mail: reservations@chobe.botsnet.bw, website: www.threecities.co.za
Kubu Lodge: PO Box 43, Kasane. Tel: +267 6250312, e-mail: kubu@botsnet.bw, website: www.kubulodge.net
Chobe Safari Lodge: PO Box 10, Kasane. Tel: +267 6250336, e-mail: reservations@chobelodge.co.bw, website: www.chobesafarilodge.com

Index

Page numbers in *italics* refer to photographs.

First published in 2007 by Struik Publishers
(a division of New Holland Publishing (South Africa) (Pty) Ltd)
New Holland Publishing is a member of Johnnic Communications Ltd

Garfield House, 86–88 Edgware Road,
London W2 2EA, United Kingdom
www.newhollandpublishers.com
80 McKenzie Street, Cape Town 8001,
South Africa www.struik.co.za
14 Aquatic Drive, Frenchs Forest,
NSW 2086, Australia
218 Lake Road, Northcote,
Auckland, New Zealand

ISBN 978 1 77007 361 6
1 3 5 7 9 10 8 6 4 2

Publishing managers: Dominique le Roux and Felicity Nyikadzino Berold
Managing editor: Lesley Hay-Whitton
Project Co-ordinator: Samantha Menezes-Fick
Editor: Hermanda Steele
Designer: Daniele Michelini
Concept designer: Alison Day
Cartographer: Tessa van Schaik
Proofreader: Sharon Dagnin
Indexer: Hermanda Steele

Reproduction by Hirt & Carter Cape (Pty) Ltd
Printed and bound by Craft Print International Ltd

Pg 154: *A temporary fishing village along the banks of the Zambezi River.*